IN
TUNEFUL ACCORD

IN
TUNEFUL ACCORD

Making Music Work in Church

JAMES WHITBOURN

First published in Great Britain 1996
Society for Promoting Christian Knowledge
Holy Trinity Church
Marylebone Road
London NW1 4DU

British Library Cataloguing-in-Publication Data

A catalogue record of this book is available
from the British Library

ISBN 0-281-04825-8

Typeset by Pioneer Associates, Perthshire
Printed in Great Britain by
The Cromwell Press, Melksham, Wiltshire

Contents

to Naomi, with love

Acknowledgements

I am indebted to a great many individuals – too numerous to name individually – who have shared their thoughts and experience in church music with me over many years. Fellow choral conductors and organists, colleagues in the Religious Broadcasting department of the BBC, members of my family and other friends have all shared with me insights about music and worship in church which have come from their own experience. I owe a good deal to Derek Baldwin, a former organist of St James's Church, Tunbridge Wells; Professor John Harper, formerly organist of Magdalen College, Oxford; and John Williams, formerly organist of the Chapel Royal, HM Tower of London; all of whom helped and taught me at an impressionable age.

Some of the thoughts in this book coincide with those expressed in a BBC Radio 3 Documentary broadcast in April 1995 which I presented, and for which I visited a number of churches with BBC colleagues Amanda Hancox and Janet McLarty.

In writing this book, I am indebted to my sister, Katherine Gregory, who helped with the preparation of the final text, and to my father, Dr Philip Whitbourn, for assisting with the drawing of architectural plans.

Finally, I am grateful to Brendan Walsh, formerly Managing Editor of SPCK, and to Rachel Boulding, Senior Editor, for their trust and encouragement towards its completion.

Preface

Churches today are faced with the most bewildering array of choices. Which services shall we use? Shall we have a choir? What about a music band? Do we need some modern songs? Can we still sing the traditional hymns? Can't we use some Taizé music? Why not mix together the old and the new? Shall we still use hymn-books or have separate sheets? Shall we appoint an organist or a director of music?

Forty years ago, clergy had to make none of these choices. Nor did congregations, church councils or musicians. Decisions were made on a different level altogether: shall the choir sing this anthem or that? Which tune do we sing to this hymn? In short, they were made *within* the system but not, generally, *about* it.

These musical questions are part of a legacy of change in public worship which the twentieth century has bequeathed to the whole Christian Church. Every decade has added weight to a cargo whose huge momentum has finally proved sufficient to alter the habits of four hundred years or more. The Liturgical Movement, as it became known, has embraced church members from almost all denominations in Europe and America, who have argued the case for active participation of the people to be restored to the official worship of the Church.

Although the changes apply to the *whole* of the worship – spoken and sung – and ended in a reordering and rewriting of entire services, consideration of the music used in worship has played a crucial role. The directions of Pope Pius X relating to church music (1903), for example, provided a significant boost, and many other matters of a musical kind since then have added to the evolution and progress of thought. It is ironic, then, that from the changes that have come about, church music has been a casualty rather than a beneficiary so far.

Throughout the 1960s, the churches were urgently and publicly redefining their primary values for public worship. They set out on a course of experimentation and debate, and began to legalize the introduction of new forms of service. After 1965, for example, a new Measure meant that the 1662 Act of Uniformity no longer governed the worship of the Church of England, and that modern services could be sanctioned. A number of new rites were brought into use, culminating in the Alternative Service Book, published in 1980. This book reflects recent study on liturgy, and especially the origins of the Eucharist, which is reordered. Most importantly for musicians, the worship is written in modern English.

Meanwhile, the Second Vatican Council (which met between 1962 and 1965) produced the new Catholic Missal of 1970, and a new Breviary the following year. Together, they involved a reordering of the Mass and the Daily Office, new Eucharistic Prayers, and rewriting all the services in the vernacular.

Had there been no music in the Church, these changes could have been effected simply, with any debate limited to purely liturgical and theological issues. In churches which do not use music, this has indeed happened: the old service books are put away, and the new books are used instead. The change-over is the work of minutes.

When there is music, nothing is so simple. The first effect of changing the words is that the bulk of the repertory (which set to music the old words) is put out of use. Then the huge structure which supported it is broken up. Musical groups are disbanded. Links with schools and other institutions are modified or discarded. Ministers, lay readers, and members of church councils and committees find themselves having to start again from scratch, making fundamental musical decisions without the benefit of centuries of wisdom.

In the 1992 report of the Archbishop's Commission on Church Music, *In Tune with Heaven*, the Anglican Church publicly admitted that there has been a problem with the standard of church music in recent years, brought about by these changes. In gentler ways, the Free Churches have also experienced change. The *Methodist Hymnbook* of 1932 was replaced by a newer and broader collection, *Hymns and Psalms*, in 1984. The United Reformed Church and the Baptists introduced new hymn-books more recently. All of them have joined the metamorphosis of taste and style which has moved through the Established Churches. Often, church leaders and decision-makers have no way of knowing whether the vision they have for their churches corresponds at all with the possibilities they present. This book is primarily for these people, as well as for some church musicians, and for that reason it is written not as a musical handbook but as a discussion of system and design. I do not touch on interpretation or performance, but stop at the point where the music is ready to be rehearsed or performed. If you like, this book finishes just as the conductor raises the baton to begin.

In 1994, I began to prepare for a Radio 3 documentary on church music by placing a notice in the *Radio Times*, asking for people's own experiences in recent years. The response was overwhelming and proved beyond doubt that certain trends and situations which I had observed were being repeated right across the country. I visited several of the churches to see things at first hand. On other occasions too, over the last decade, I have seen a good many parish choirs and music groups in Britain and abroad at close quarters. All of these choirs and instrumentalists are gathered together into the fictitious musicians of the cathedral and parish churches quoted in this book. In many cases I have referred to their musicians as 'he'; every time it must be assumed that the pronoun could equally well be – and often is, in reality – 'she'.

Much of my own experience has been within the Anglican Church, and my perspective doubtless reflects that fact. I believe, however, that the Catholic Church in England and Churches of other denominations have gone through similar processes of liturgical and musical change in recent years, and that this book applies equally to any branch of the Christian Church.

Introduction

Barchester Today

A lot has changed in Barchester. It is now a century and a half since the novelist Anthony Trollope first began his story of life in its cathedral close. The same period has elapsed since his contemporary Samuel Sebastian Wesley wrote his withering account of sacred music of the era: 'No cathedral in this country', he said, 'possesses at this day, a musical force competent to embody and give effect to the evident intentions of the Church with regard to music' (*A Few Words on Cathedral Music and the Musical System of the Church with a Plan of Reform*, 1849). In other words, had Barchester been any more than fiction, its cathedral choir would have been in a very sorry state. What S. S. Wesley recognized was the importance of what he describes as 'the musical system of the Church'. His plan for reform makes much mention of musicians' salaries, but talks also of the provision of music copies by a resident copyist and the management of choirboys. He discusses the systematic use of deputies for absent choirmen, and methods for training boys (whose voices, incidentally, he points out 'are a poor substitute for the vastly superior quality and power of those of women').

Since Wesley's day things have improved, and almost *every* cathedral in England now possesses the musical force which he longed to see. Today, we may assume that the cathedral choir at Barchester is flourishing. But down the road, the story is different.

1

For the sake of argument, let us add some other churches to Trollope's city: St Mary's, St Peter's and (just outside Barchester) St Swithun's. A few facts and figures about the churches are set out below.

These churches have experienced a liturgical revolution which has bypassed the cathedral, and a huge gulf separates their styles and traditions. St Mary's, for example, has become so different now that it is hard to see how they were ever related.

This book is about the musical system of the Church today (and tomorrow), applied not only to cathedrals, which are currently in good shape, but to all churches. In Barchester, what the cathedral has been able to keep is a healthy system which serves their chosen style of music well. There are elements of the system which apply equally to any church, even if the styles of music and worship within them are radically different. This book is about the people of Barchester who have found things hard in recent years and who are struggling to find solutions. It is for all people who have to make choices for their churches, and who want to create the systems which will make their choices work.

St Mary's Barchester

Situation. Imposing church in centre of city. It is the largest parish church in Barchester.

Building. Fine 15th century church with some important early glass. Bell tower.

Congregation. Sunday congregation of about 150. Much used during the week for civic and city functions. Some 15 local firms have links with the church for annual services, especially at Christmas.

Sunday Services. 8.00 am Holy Communion (BCP); 10.30 am Family Worship; 6.30 pm Evening Prayer.

Worship. Church of England, evangelical but with very traditional roots. Heavy emphasis on preaching and host to several well-known visiting preachers each year.

Music. Until 1987, St Mary's supported a large choir of men and boys. Most boys came from the cathedral school, a few from other local schools. The choir was disbanded after a major review of the worship by PCC and a reordering of the church. The organist resigned and many of the choir left the church altogether. Several volunteers have kept the music going, with a small group of singers and instrumentalists, none of them very accomplished. The actions of the choir and organist after the review left a bad taste for many years, and music has not been a high priority since. From the money saved on music since 1987, a half-time director of music's salary has been funded, and the first holder has recently been appointed. After two years the post will be reviewed. Current music group consists of violin, cello, oboe, clarinet and horn, 6 singers and keyboard player. There is a fine 3-manual Harrison organ.

Rector. Canon Michael Withytt BA, AKC. Much-liked figure in Barchester. Approachable and interested in town events. He came to Barchester 5 years ago. No musical training, but a keen sense of its importance in worship. He hopes to see things developing fast now.

3

Director of Music. Rebecca Mortone ARCM. Newly appointed to pick up the pieces after years of neglect. Hopes to develop instrumental ensemble. Good organist. Teaches music. Starts next week.

St Peter's Barchester

Situation. Centrally placed, but slightly further than St Mary's from the business and shopping area of Barchester.

Building. Also of 15th century origin, but not as large or as fine as St Mary's. Attractive and worth a visit, nonetheless.

Congregation. Sunday congregation of 75–100. Not often used during the week.

Sunday Services. 10.00 am Parish Communion; 6.30 pm Evensong (BCP with choir 1st Sunday of the month); otherwise ASB.

Worship. Church of England. Middle-of-the-road, but with High Church background. Elegant liturgy and good preaching. Lively congregation.

Music. Choir of 24 voices: men, women, girls and boys, aged

4

between 6 and 80. Good-sized repertoire. The choir sings one charity concert in the cathedral each year, which is well attended.

Rector. Revd Peter Goodman MA. Good New Testament scholar and fine preacher. Well liked by the congregation, but not a familiar sight around Barchester. A former chorister, he is an active supporter of the choir.

Organist and Choirmaster. Richard Singer ALCM. A civil engineer by profession, he is a good organist and a well-respected choir trainer. He is greatly helped by the choir secretary, Rosie Day, whose husband and two daughters also sing in the choir.

St Swithun's Upper Barchester

Situation. A country parish, 3 miles from Barchester.

Building. Small and undistinguished. Late 19th century.

Congregation. Sundays about 50. Always locked during the week.

Sunday Services. 8.00 am Communion; 10.30 am Morning Prayer; 6.30 pm (1st Sunday of the month only) Evening Praise.

Music. Elderly choir of 8 voices, all of them 'survivors' of a flourishing choir which has gradually declined over the past 10 years. There have been no new members during that period. There is also a folk group of 3 guitars, piano and 8 singers. A rock band of 5 young people play at the monthly evening service.

Worship. Church of England. Services are freely adapted from ASB. They are conducted without much style, and the preaching is often mediocre.

Vicar. Revd Don Muddle. Non-stipendiary minister. A retired local government official with a late calling to the ministry. He works hard for the parish, but he lives 15 miles away, so he is rarely seen other than on Sundays.

Organist. St Swithun's has been without an organist for some time. Mrs Grimshaw plays the organ most Sundays, but she readily admits that she is a pianist, and would prefer to give up when she is 80 next year. John and Carol Summers lead the folk group and co-ordinate most of the music.

Barchester Cathedral

Situation. The focal point of the historic centre of Barchester.

Building. 12th century origin and one of the finest English cathedrals. Built on a grand scale with an imposing central tower.

Congregation. About 20 regulars for weekday Evensong, plus between 40 and 100 visitors. For Sunday morning Eucharist, a regular congregation of 400.

Services. Morning Prayer and Holy Communion are said daily. Choral Evensong is sung daily except Wednesdays, when it is said. The Sung Eucharist is the principal Sunday Service.

Worship. Church of England. Morning Prayer and Holy Communion are ASB. Choral Evensong is BCP.

Music. Fine choir of 18 boys and 12 men, conducted by the Organist and Master of the Choristers. There is an Assistant Organist and an Organ Scholar. The boys are all educated on scholarships at the cathedral school, and most of them board. There is a large 4-manual organ.

Dean. Very Revd Michael Parsons. Known for his recent television series *Journey to God.* He manages the clergy of the Chapter well but does not interfere with the choir. Some see him as aloof. The Precentor is responsible for the music, and she is very supportive of the choral foundation, and a good listener and pastor to choirmen, boys and choristers' parents.

Organist. Simon Morgan MA, FRCO, ARCM. Outstanding organist and choirmaster. Also conducts Barchester Choral Society and is well respected as a conductor by local orchestras.

PART I

A Time and a Place

This section discusses the way music fits into the Christian tradition of public worship, and looks at the factors which are to be considered before drawing up a musical plan for a church

CHAPTER 1

Away from Solitude: Music in Public Worship

A basic contradiction threatens to close this book before it is even opened. Is there any such thing as 'Christian music'? To speak of Christian *love* is one thing: Jesus taught his followers tirelessly about the true meaning of love. To speak of Christian *healing* or Christian *preaching* makes sense too: Jesus set an example which others can follow. Compared with these, the term *Christian music* seems an imposition on someone for whom music appears to be frustratingly unimportant. Christ was not a musician, and even his teaching on public prayer and worship, pieced together from the Gospels, seems to give little encouragement to the tradition of church worship which has dominated this millennium:

> When you pray, you must not be like the hypocrites; for they love to stand and pray in the synagogues and at the street corners, that they may be seen by men. Truly, I say to you, they have received their reward. But when you pray, go into your room and shut your door and pray to your Father who is in secret; and your Father who sees in secret will reward you (Matt. 6.5–6).

When Jesus prays to the Father, it is in solitude. Even when his disciples are with him, as in the garden of Gethsemane, Jesus prays in their presence, but not *with* them:

11

And they went to a place which was called Gethsemane; and he said to his disciples, 'Sit here, while I pray' (Mark 14.32).

The secret and solitary prayer which Jesus commends to his followers contrasts dramatically with the type of celebration King David had arranged two or three hundred years earlier:

David commanded the chiefs of the Levites to appoint their brethren as the singers who should play loudly on musical instruments, on harps and lyres and cymbals, to raise sounds of joy. Chenaniah, leader of the Levites in music, should direct the music, for he understood it. So all Israel brought up the ark of the covenant of the Lord with shouting, to the sound of the horn, trumpets, and cymbals, and made loud music on harps and lyres (1 Chron. 15.16, 22, 28).

On the face of it, Jesus's teaching is in opposition to the public ceremonial tradition of God's people. By implication, the bands of musicians are also in jeopardy. Chenaniah's successors might have feared for their jobs. On the other hand, Jesus taught in the synagogue, and, according to St Luke, he worshipped in the synagogue every Sabbath, sometimes reading the Scripture aloud (Luke 4.16). Even as a small boy, Jesus called the temple in Jerusalem 'my Father's house'. His presence and teaching in the synagogues suggests that he expected his followers to worship regularly in the synagogues as well, and his instructions and example in prayer need to be read in this light: they are not complete instructions in themselves, but rather a supplement to the religious practice which is already in place – a 'Christian supplement', you could say, to the Jewish tradition. With worship and ceremony, presumably, the same can be inferred.

In Jewish tradition, music was an impressive and sophisticated part of the temple ceremonial, with well-ordered choirs and musicians. In this sense, Christian music does not begin with Christ; as with prayer, worship and the study of Scripture, it begins long before his time on earth. The fact that Jesus does not mention the importance of music, therefore, does *not* mean that it is unimportant; rather, it seems to require no particular supplement to the long musical tradition which already belongs to the people of God. In a roundabout way, therefore, the practice of ceremonial music is endorsed by Christ.

Why Have Music in Church?

Let us set aside for a moment any specific churches, such as those at Barchester, and consider the way music affects the whole Christian Church.

The Church is the body of people who have a common belief in Christ the Messiah. Within it, there are several different uses for music: it can be used in worship, as a way of honouring and revering God; it can be used as a means of strengthening a fraternity (Christians call this 'fellowship'); or it can be used as a way of attracting others in order to enlarge the fraternity ('evangelism').

Labels apart, there are good reasons to distinguish between the various uses of music. In the same way that the intended recipient of any letter, whatever the subject, will radically alter its content and presentation, so it is with music. Think, for example, of the uproar among the residents of a small village when they hear that a new road is to be built through the middle of the village. Letters are written in abundance, one letter to a government official, another to the group fighting the new road, the next to the planners. There is an 'open' letter addressed to a national newspaper, to be read by people of differing views and positions of possible influence, and finally there is a private letter written to a friend. Although the subject is common to all, the styles of language and presentation of each letter are very different. The one to the government arrives on headed paper ('Dear Sir, I should like to draw your attention to a damaging proposal . . .'). For the people fighting against the road, there are words to stir them into action ('This road is an outrage which will completely ruin our village . . .'). The open letter is written in combative style to engage and entertain as well as to persuade, while the personal letter shows something of the human feelings ('It makes me cry to think of our beautiful village being ruined . . .').

Just as the sender knows who the recipient will be, so the Church must know who is being addressed in order to find the right form of address. Essentially, Christians can speak to God, they can speak to each other and they can speak to other people. This is what is meant by those terms 'worship', 'fellowship' and 'evangelism'.

Music as Worship

Music is a part of the tradition of sacrificial worship, in which people come to church to offer to God the best they have. It is different from other forms of art, such as painting or sculpture: bound by time, it can exist only by the constant involvement of human beings. With music there is a double offering: its own worth and beauty is recognized as a gift, but it is also a medium through which a sacrifice is made by those who perform it. Today, in churches throughout the world, choirs train and rehearse intensively together to achieve the highest possible standards of music with which to embellish daily worship. It is prepared and performed in just as practised a manner regardless of the number of people in the congregation. The skill, talent and work of those who contribute to it is simply offered to God by them, on behalf of all members of the church.

Music for Fellowship

Music may be used in a church as a uniting force which joins together a body of people in song. The idea of a singing fraternity is not confined to the church: there are school songs which bring pupils together in an atmosphere of solidarity; there are songs which football and rugby fans sing lustily at matches; there are national anthems which stir up feelings of patriotism, and there are songs for clubs, unions and political parties, which forge a common bond.

The drawback is that it works only when the songs are known to everybody. Not many are. If a song is known by only half the people, it can have the most divisive and exclusive effect. The people who join in are unconsciously saying, 'We are the inner group and we have an even greater solidarity.' Fellowship then swiftly turns to schism.

Music in Evangelism

Music may be used in church principally as a means of attracting people into it. The worth of the music is judged then by its immediacy and appeal and is chosen specifically with the contemporary human ear in mind. In addition, evangelistic music is likely to be used outside the usual meeting places for Christians and may embrace styles which are not normally used in church. In other words, the worth of the music is defined not by a detached judgement of the music's own musical merits, but by its appeal to the majority of those who hear it. In religious jargon, music is acting as an evangelistic tool.

Its use, however, is notoriously difficult to predict. It is an ironic fact that a person with strongly-held beliefs who expresses them clearly and simply is usually more impressive than someone who compromises them in an attempt to match your own. This is equally true outside the realm of religious belief. If someone says, 'I think Mozart is the greatest composer', and talks about the music he loves, you can respect that view. Even if you do not share his love of Mozart's music, his enthusiasm for it will have a drawing power. Suppose he happens to know that you are not a fan. He says, 'I agree that not all Mozart's music is very good, but I think that some pieces are at least worth listening to.' In an attempt to meet you halfway, he has watered down his own conviction, and lost his evangelistic drive.

The assumption that people want what they already have is not a sound evangelistic philosophy. In the 1990s, for example, the commercial popularity among non-churchgoers of sixteenth-century polyphonic music such as the music of Victoria and Palestrina, and of Gregorian chant has surprised many people within the Church who had dismissed the repertory as 'irrelevant' or 'out of touch'. One Spanish recording of Gregorian chant has sold literally millions of copies world-wide and reached the top of the Spanish charts. This was not the intention of the monks who made it, and part of its attraction is the single-minded devotion to God which runs through it and is audible in the music.

Music for All Seasons and All Reasons

Sometimes two or three purposes of music combine at once. The Spanish monks, for example, sing a plainchant as an act of communal worship. As they do so, their bonds of fraternity are strengthened by their common purpose in worship. As it happens, a pilgrim who has entered the church is deeply moved by the sound of the singing, and decides to learn more about the teaching of Christ. The music is intended as worship, but it has overtones of fellowship and evangelism as well.

The addition of music to words blurs the edges in other ways. One text will be a prayer or an expression of thanks addressed to God. Another will be a scriptural narrative such as the story of the birth of Christ which is described in the hymn 'Once in Royal David's City', or a straightforward statement of fraternity, such as the 1970s song 'We are come into His house', in which Christians clearly address each other rather than God.

When the same words are set to music, however, they are directed in a different way. Take the sentence, 'Let us come into his presence with thanksgiving.' It is an invitation to worship, addressed to other Christians, rather than to God, in the language of a fraternity. A composer sets it to music, and it is sung by a small choir at the beginning of a service. For them it becomes an act of sacrificial worship. It is not the words which are their offering, but their time, talents and musicianship.

Faith and Religion

From the relationship between words themselves and the way they are expressed emerges the distinction between one person's faith and another person's religion.

When Paul, James and the other New Testament authors wrote their Epistles, for example, they were clearly addressed to specific churches and individuals. For that reason they contained particular advice, some of which is not directly relevant to anyone else. Yet still these letters are recognized as words which nourish the faith of subsequent generations of believers. So how have those personal letters come to influence so many?

Consider Paul's letter to the Galatians, which stems from Paul's uncontainable faith in Christ Jesus. The Christians in Galatia had received Paul with great friendliness: they had received him as their guest with pleasure and accepted his gospel as a message from God. Churches were formed and were running well. Yet after a second visit, Paul is astonished to find how quickly things have turned away from his gospel. From this crisis, he writes a critical letter which he hopes will set them back on the path they had been on before.

Later, the letter is collected into the New Testament, it is translated into other languages and eventually divided into chapters and verses. Some centuries after it is written, portions are being read or sung in churches in an organized way - a number of verses each day of the week. A verse is set to music. As it is sung, it is repeated and remembered, and becomes part of a religious observance which builds the faith of a Christian believer two thousand years on.

17

The relationship between faith and religion, then, begins to work in a cyclic way: from faith come the boundaries of religion – doctrine and belief. The religion then begins to build up faith, and link together generations of believers from different cultures and traditions.

So although they are inextricably linked, faith and religion are not the same thing. Religion expresses faith in an ordered way. By organized repetition, it nourishes the faith on which it is built.

Music and Words

For a person of faith, any words or none at all may be used as a means of communicating with God. In religion, however, words are gathered into poetry, prose and prayer, and arranged in a systematic way (or 'liturgy') so that they may be used time and time again. Through repetition, they become part of a common religious experience.

Translated into musical terms, this means that any sounds or none may be used as part of a genuine dialogue with God, but that in liturgy they conform to a system. Whatever sounds are used, however, clearly none is a substitute for faith. Music in religion can lead to faith, it can build up faith, but it cannot *be* faith. All the discussion and comment in this book must be seen in that context. Music is an important part of religion, but it is no more. Paradoxically for an art which claims importance, it is entirely dispensable; only if it is *chosen* to play a part in religious life does it acquire any importance. If that does happen, though, music has the power to nurture belief, shape a faith and influence human life.

Guidelines from the Bible

The responsibility for designing the systems of the Christian religion has fallen to believers of each generation, with the help and inspiration of those before them. On the subject of liturgy, the New Testament is almost silent, and with the exception of a commandment of Jesus made to his followers at the Last Supper, to 'do this in remembrance of me', barely any instruction whatever comes from Jesus as to how the members of his Church should worship God when they gather together in his name.

In many ways this is a helpful and healthy responsibility. Were the letter to be laid down by divine law, liturgy would quickly take on the character of a pagan ritual, with unquestioning obedience to an unchangeable set of rules which must not be broken. But since no specific requirement is made by God as to the style and form his worship should take, it is up to believers themselves to see that what they do for him is worth doing at all.

Rock of Ages or Age of Rock?

Until a decade or two ago, there was a general acceptance in Britain as to what music was suitable for use in church and what was not. This has been widely questioned in recent years, and the whole matter placed under scrutiny. New questions are now asked about differing tastes in musical style, and how to respond to them.

It is difficult to find consensus of taste within any group of people, whether or not they are part of a church. At Barchester Books, for example, the manager, Vanessa, is leaving the shop after seventeen years. Susan, her closest friend at work, is asked to choose a gift on behalf of everyone. She chooses a blue vase which she knows Vanessa will like. Some of the others like it, but others think it is hideous. All of them are happy with the choice, however, because Susan has chosen it, and she knows Vanessa best. Come the presentation, though, Vanessa decides to thank everybody one by one. 'I think it is beautiful,' she says to Philip, who thinks it is hideous. He shuffles and mutters, 'We thought you would like it.' The vase has been given to Vanessa on Philip's behalf, even though he dislikes it. He feels uncomfortable not because he is unhappy with the gift, but merely because it is not to his own taste.

When it comes to worship, taste plays an important part. This time, no one has the insight to know which style of music is most pleasing to God, or even whether there is any preference at all. But it remains true that there is an uncomfortable feeling which people experience when they cannot embrace as their own what is being offered on their behalf.

A few years ago the repertoire of choral and organ music built up by the Victorians and succeeding generations was one such source of discomfort, felt by those who found this music alien to their taste. They found the hymns sentimental and the anthems long and over-romantic. Their taste prevented their own involvement in its offering.

Spoilt for Choice

Since then, a revolution in church music has introduced the largest ever range of styles used at any one time, the tables are turned, and both comfort and discomfort is felt, to varying degrees, on all sides.

As with the introduction of new liturgies, Christians have not always understood those who subscribe to differing tastes. Those who yearn for some popular-style expression of their faith have often sneered at those who clamour for the 'fossilized' music of the past, just as the others poke fun at the 'happy clappy brigade' who seem to be throwing out their religious inheritance. Regrettable though this is, it may be understood up to a point, and all comes back to the relationship between faith and religion. Faith begins with a spark of divine revelation. Often it is tiny and unsustainable against the counter-attacks of questioning and derision. But that spark of faith is nurtured by religion, an ordering of prayer and praise, in which small parts of the faiths of many are combined to create something much bigger than that of a single believer. Its dimensions are those of width and breadth. Those who live by it give it depth.

For Anglicans brought up in the 1960s there were few choices to be made. The 1662 Prayer Book liturgy represented the universal language of the Anglican Church, which expresses the divine nature of God in its particular way. This was their religion, and it helped them instruct their faith. Not only the liturgy, but the music, the social functions and all the trappings, were part of it.

In no time at all, everything is in doubt. Some see limitations in the language and style. The most ardent reformers go further: they pronounce that this liturgy, and all that goes with it, cannot be tolerated any longer. For hundreds and thousands of Christians, therefore, the religion that they have learnt from the Church, and upon which they have slowly built their faith, is being disowned by those who once preached it. The foundations of faith, it seems, are under fire.

Look at it then from another point of view, that of a new believer with a spark of faith but, as yet, no religion. Hers is a divine revelation of a living Spirit: the discovery that the presence of God is a contemporary rather than a merely historical phenomenon. As she begins to search for religious roots, she finds that what was revealed to her in faith is immediately contradicted by the religion. The words and the music she hears have an ancient ring, and seem to belong to a culture to which she does not belong. She finds that the religion is, after all, predominantly historical, and she has nothing to support her faith.

In the end, a preference for musical style comes down to taste and cultural upbringing, not doctrine. But it contributes to religious experience and understanding to such a degree that it has the capacity to make or break religion, and thus to influence the development of Christian belief.

21

Only the Best

The fact that no particular style of music is ordained of God for the Christian Church has an important bearing on musical quality, both in composition and performance. It is the responsibility of a church to see to it that what they intended to offer is what is actually being offered to God. If you promise a person a hand-made cut-glass vase, and immediately present them with one which is chipped and broken, the gift, far from causing pleasure, gives offence. Perhaps it would have been better to give nothing at all. In the case of a musical offering to God, the promise is made when the music is chosen; the offering is made when it is performed.

If Christians decide to worship God by singing a psalm to a responsorial setting, they must see that it is properly done. If the chanting falls apart and ends in chaos, it would have been better to worship another way.

Easier Said Than Done

In music, however, it is easier to decide what ought to be done than it is to do it. It is a fact that it is much simpler to describe music than it is to perform it. To say, 'We ought to make this piece lively and exuberant' is one thing: to achieve a lively result in performance is another. It is easy to say 'We want to use these sounds to create a devotional atmosphere', but it is hard to do so. So it is with musical policy in a church: we may say, 'We want to achieve variety', without knowing how this may be done. Since choices must be made, it is important that they be informed choices, and that whatever sounds are chosen for God, they are within the capability of those who give them.

Choosing music for God demands a combination of judgement and skill. The balance of these two qualities changes from one historical period to another, and we have recently come through a period when little emphasis was placed on choice and judgement, and a great deal was placed on skill. The choice of musical resource up until the 1970s was uniform and limited, but the standards of musical performance were high. That picture has since been reversed, and the picture now is of a huge range and diversity of music, much of it performed to a very low standard. There are signs that churches are looking for a new balance now, as they wade through the undergrowth searching for the sounds to offer God.

Making music work in practice comes from making the *right* musical choices and judgements, and subsequently gathering them together in a systematic way. The best chance of making them comes when the physical and practical realities of music are understood and taken into account. Now is the time to return to the churches of Barchester and look at the facts and figures of the buildings and those who worship within them. Once that is done, those people can plan how to organize themselves, and make their music fulfil whatever ideals of worship, fellowship and evangelism they have chosen.

CHAPTER 2

Music and the Building

Along the road from St Peter's stands the newly-built Barchester Arts Centre, a monument to modern design. The City of Barchester Chamber Orchestra (CBCO) has its home there and they give concerts two or three times each month. For the rest of the time, anything can happen. Sometimes there is a solo singer, sometimes a string quartet, a pianist or a brass band. There are jazz quartets, small operas are staged, and the hall is used for lectures and conferences too. This was always the plan, and when the hall was built, the architects brought in acoustic engineers. They wanted a space which could accommodate as many different combinations as possible.

At St Peter's it is a different story. Only the church choir and congregation sing there. It is true that they go off once a year to sing the charity concert at the cathedral, but essentially St Peter's choir is a 'resident' group of musicians. The church, as it happens, is very good for singing. It has a warm reverberance which seems to help the choir.

The relationship between the church building and its musicians is fixed, and it is all the more important, therefore, to match the two in an appropriate way. Now and again at the Arts Centre you go to a concert at which the performers are not well matched to the hall. You find a solo singer cannot be heard well because his voice is not big enough for the space, or else you find the brass section of an orchestra is overwhelming because the room is too small. The hall manager takes comfort from the fact that the following day an entirely different ensemble will be there, and puts the one-off failure down to experience. Church musicians, on the other hand, work not by one-off occasions, but by regular services week after week, and whatever choices are made for their building will affect the church's worship for many years.

The Constant and the Changing

One of the difficulties experienced by congregations is that, in most instances, their church was designed and built by worshippers belonging to an earlier generation. Often congregations inherit a building which is several centuries old. Whatever spiritual value is derived from its age and history, it remains a source of tension within many churches. Buildings of solid construction do not lend themselves to change, especially when there are features of artistic and historical merit. People, on the other hand, change constantly. In the course of, say, fifty years, it is likely that almost the entire congregation will have altered, bringing with them new fashions and tastes.

The friction is not always obvious, but it becomes noticeable when contrasted with a church where the match of building and people has *not* shifted significantly. Time spent in one of the working monasteries, for example, where the way of life of the community has remained as constant as the building in which they gather, demonstrates the degree of harmony between congregation and place of worship which can exist. In this case, a church built five hundred years ago is still being used in exactly the way that was first intended. For most churches, though, the building and the people represent a distinction between that which is constant and that which is changing.

Family Pews

This tension – or lack of it – applies not only to the buildings themselves, but to the furniture within them – the pews, stalls and galleries. The same restrictions apply often, especially where there are items of artistic or historic importance. Walk into the quire area of any of the English medieval cathedrals, and you will see a set of choir-stalls, usually raised slightly above the level of the others, and sometimes set slightly forward. They were designed to accommodate a group of singers of a particular size, and typically, the sizes of choirs since their foundation have changed very little. Consequently, the stalls originally provided for them continue to serve as convenient and practical furnishings.

This is not always the case in other churches, however. Mr Lowe sings bass, but he is about to leave the choir of Barchester Cathedral. The organist has already advertised his job and will be auditioning five people next Tuesday. None of the candidates comes from Barchester, but all are willing to move to the city if they are offered the post. In return, there is a house, a salary, and the opportunity to teach at the choir school. Down the road at St Peter's, meanwhile, Richard Singer, the organist, is bracing himself for the loss of young Barry, who is going off to college. When he leaves, he knows he will be a bass short unless someone new joins the church or he can persuade one of the two men who used to sing in the choir (but left because of leading the youth group) back into the fold. Then, along comes a new soprano. Where shall she sit? She cannot sit where Barry used to sit, because that was in the back row with the basses. But the front pew is already full. Richard thinks how much easier it would be if the pews could be moved to accommodate the singers he actually had, rather than those his predecessors might once have had.

Now to the other side of town, to St Mary's, where they have a small instrumental ensemble. The sad news there is that Jane, their clarinettist, is moving away. The hope on the horizon, though, is the rumour that the new curate's son plays the trumpet, so he might be joining them before too long.

What a contrast with the CBCO. When they lose a clarinettist they advertise for a replacement clarinettist. They would never

26

make an open advertisement for any instrumentalist, or say 'clarinettist preferred'. Consequently, the orchestral layout, system and structure remains the same.

The influence of either a building or its furniture may seem a petty consideration when it comes to the music in a church, and it may be outrageous to suggest, or appear to suggest, that something as living and vibrant as music should in any way be influenced by something as static as pews or wooden stalls. The fact remains, though, that the furniture in a church is of great practical significance to music-making, and just as the chamber orchestra requires a certain space in which to rehearse and perform, laid out in a particular way, so also do instrumentalists and singers in a church, if their endeavours are to be successful.

If religion is a systematic presentation of faith, then the music which serves it must also follow a systematic path. Systems create structures, and structures are more difficult to change than ideas are to create, just as buildings change more slowly than the people who inhabit them. This is a tension which needs to be recognized so that its effect does not begin to spill over into the life of a church and start to destroy rather than create.

Where Do I Sit?

Sound, like light, is directional. Hold out your hand halfway between a ceiling light and the floor. A shadow will appear, because the direct light waves between the bulb and the floor have been blocked. The area of shadow, however, will not be an area of total pitch darkness; it will still be lit, but less intensely, by reflected, rather than direct, light. The same is true of sound: if a singer has her back to you and sings a note you will hear the note as it reaches you from whatever reflective surfaces are available. But if she turns towards you, you will hear it with greater clarity.

This simple fact is often disregarded in the making of music in churches. Even if it is not actually ignored, it is sometimes optimistically hoped that the usual physical properties of sound will somehow fail to apply to a particular church, and that singers or instrumentalists turned away from the congregation will nevertheless be clearly heard.

We need to think again of the purpose of the music in the church. Is it worship, fellowship or evangelism? There is almost bound to be a difference in the way musicians are ideally placed, according to the type of music being performed, and for whom.

Fitting People In

At the Cathedral

The singers at Barchester Cathedral are arranged into two equal choirs, positioned to face each other. This layout is known as the collegiate arrangement. Each of the two choirs has a balance of treble, alto, tenor and bass voices. Sometimes they sing alternately, while for other parts of the service they sing together.

For the cathedral, this layout is very practical: it means that when the two choirs are singing separately, they are singing towards each other. They can hear the other side well enough to take their cues, and when there are not many people in the congregation, they are spared the uncomfortable practice of singing into an empty space.

The organ is the only instrument which is regularly used to accompany services, and this is situated above the screen between the two sides of the choir, making up the third side of an open rectangle (see Figure 1).

This becomes an area known as the quire (or choir), and is separated from the rest of the cathedral church by partitions or screens. In this quire area, the people of Barchester who come to services sit in the pews to either side of the choir. Although they may hear one side more clearly than the other, both sides can be clearly heard because it is a small and enclosed space. Mrs Philpot, who goes to Evensong every Thursday, prefers to sit

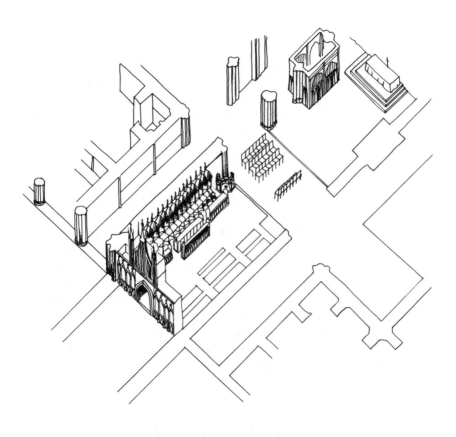

Figure 1. Quire area of Barchester Cathedral

further away, at the crossing, where she hears less directional sound from the choir, and more of the cathedral's famous acoustic.

At St Peter's

The collegiate arrangement has been emulated in parish churches which belong to the particular periods of ecclesiastical fashion, such as the medieval and Victorian eras, when the provision of a chancel was popular. St Peter's is the perfect example. The collegiate arrangement, however, applies only to the choir and not to the congregation. Furthermore, the choir is placed at one end of the church and is hidden away from the congregation by the medieval wooden rood screen. The two parts of the choir are placed at right angles to the congregation (see Figure 2) and sing towards each other but not towards the congregation. At one time, the *raison d'être* of the choir at St Peter's was to sing for regular services as an act of sacrificial worship, and in this context the layout worked. Now, the policy has shifted a little, and music is chosen more to promote unity and fellowship. Five congregational settings of the Eucharist have been introduced, for example, which are used in rotation. People in the congregation find the choir rather remote these days, tucked away behind the screen, out of sight and angled away from the congregation. They find the sound is diffused and difficult to hear.

At St Mary's

St Mary's also has choir-stalls in the chancel, but the choir has been disbanded and an instrumental group has taken its place. When the church was reordered, the front pews of the nave were removed, and a platformed area put in where a moveable altar now sits (see Figure 3). The PCC tried hard to have the choir-stalls removed, but they could not get a faculty to do so. They are a beautiful set of medieval stalls with a complete set of misericords

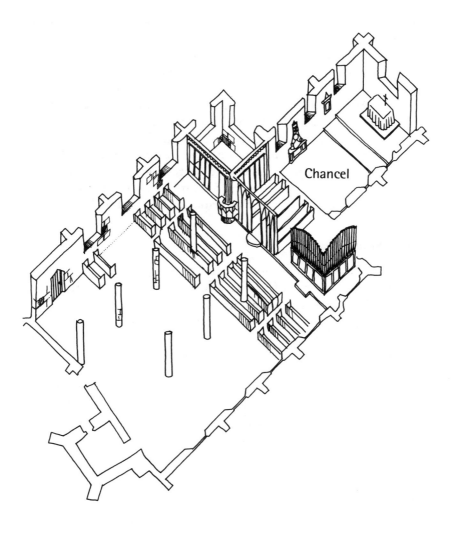

Figure 2. Inside St Peter's Barchester: chancel and nave

bearing important carvings of animals and monsters. The PCC had wanted to place the choir (which they had at the time) in the chancel, but looking west, towards the congregation, and facing the new altar. As it is, they are left with stalls but no choir. The stalls are not really suitable for the instrumentalists, who need both hands to play their instruments, and therefore also require music stands. At present there are only five of them, and they manage to fit, in pairs, between the two front pews. The cello and violin are at the front, with the oboe and clarinet behind and the horn at the back. The horn player, however, cannot hear the cello and violin at all, and the arrangement is proving very difficult. They have often talked about coming forwards onto the platform, but this area is needed for preaching and for family church activities.

At St Swithun's

St Swithun's is a small church with limited space, but of the three churches it is the most flexible. There is a small set of choir-stalls in the chancel, which are plenty big enough for the eight singers who occupy them (see Figure 4). The church has very little rever-berance, so the choir can easily be heard. In fact, people sometimes wish they were a bit further away! St Swithun's has never had any other fixed pews, and the moveable chairs have proved a great advantage for the folk group. The front four rows on the south side have simply been taken away, with a few chairs turned round for the band. They are usually half angled towards the congrega-tion, and can position themselves wherever they can hear best.

Fitting Instruments In

All the churches in Barchester possess an organ, probably the largest musical instrument. When the organ at St Swithun's was cleaned, and temporarily removed from its usual siting, the con-gregation was astounded by the size and complexity of even a

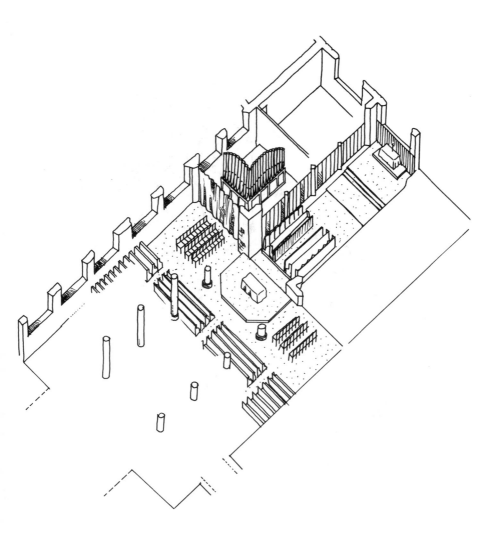

Figure 3. Inside St Mary's Barchester

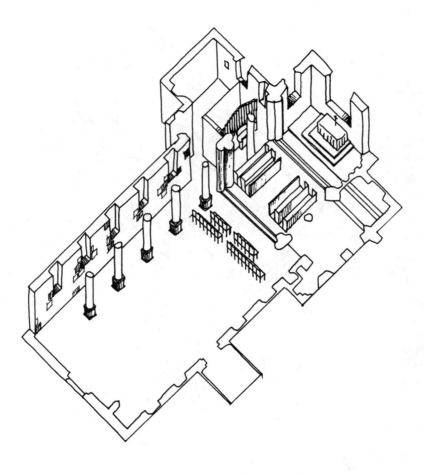

Figure 4. Inside St Swithun's Barchester

small two-manual instrument. But the organ is the musical equiv-alent of the fitted kitchen: it is an instrument of flexible shape and size which can be built into any available space, and it is often space which governs its ultimate size.

Other musical instruments are more like the free-standing kitchen units. You have to make sure not only that they fit in themselves, but that the drawers pull out or that you can still get to the cupboard when the doors are open. When instruments are used, space is needed not only for standing or sitting, but also for arm movement or any extra tools such as music stands or a wooden 'T' to prevent the cello spike from damaging the floor.

The solutions found will differ greatly according to the size of the church, the present arrangement of the furniture, and the musical ambitions of a given congregation or church.

The Music of Stone

Every enclosed space possesses acoustic properties which have a vital bearing upon sound. The acoustics depend upon the size of the enclosed space, its shape and the material which is used to enclose it. Generally speaking, the harder and flatter the surface, the more reflective it will be to sound. Thus, a wooden floor will reflect comparatively little sound, whereas a shiny marble floor will reflect sound waves well. The more surfaces in the building which are made of hard reflective surfaces, the more sound will be bounced round it. If a space is enclosed entirely by material of high reflective surface, then the sound waves will travel round the space many times before they die. This can make for either a muddled sound or a beautiful one, depending upon the ratio of the size of the building to the quality of the reflective material. Since sound travels relatively slowly (much slower than light), it will take some time to work its way round a large building, and the size of the sound wave (and therefore its volume) will have decreased significantly by the time it returns to its starting point. If it comes back too quickly, the reflected sound is too loud, and the effect can be very confusing. A gentle return, on the other hand, can enhance the quality of the music immeasurably. The way in which a building continues sound is known as its reverberance.

The sound properties of a building are part of the music and its performance. It has a bearing upon three out of the four basic elements of music, those of timbre, rhythm and volume, although none on the fourth, pitch. When a note is played within a given space, reflected sounds are added to the original, and the combination creates a new sound altogether. It is generally accepted, for example, that in a large, resonant building, the sound of a group of singers is more beautiful than it would be in a small room with no natural reverberation.

The rhythm is also changed. In a small building, a choir stops singing and there is silence. In a large resonant building, they stop singing and the sound continues. Strictly speaking it is more likely to be the speed of a piece which is affected rather than its relative rhythm, although the two go hand in hand. The volume is increased because of the extra reflected sounds which are all heard simultaneously.

The physical sound properties of a building, therefore, should be recognized as part of the music. These properties are specific and largely unchangeable, and therefore restrictive. Once again, a clear recognition of this avoids the search for the unattainable, and tends to encourage those involved to work in partnership with the building and not against it. A church with a long resonant acoustic may lend itself perfectly to Gregorian chant, but leave the music of a rock band an incomprehensible muddle. In a small carpeted church with a low wooden ceiling, a piece of Gregorian chant may make no impact at all, and may therefore be judged unsuitable for that building.

As with the positioning of musicians, it is important not to be unreasonably wishful, but rather to accept that the acoustic properties of a building are as they are, and use them to good effect.

A Time and a Place

The sight and smell of a pasta dish in Florence is quite something. You walk in from the busy street to a restaurant where they make the pasta fresh. In the background you can see the eggs and flour being mixed together and churned out into delicious strips. Back home, you walk into the supermarket and pick up a plastic packet. 'A taste of Tuscany', it announces, 'Fresh pasta made in Italy'. Somehow it doesn't seem quite the same.

Some types of music are similarly tied up with the ambience and spirituality of a particular place, and, to some extent, part of a complete 'package'. Visitors to the French community at Taizé never fail to be moved by the depth of spirituality to be found there. The music composed at Taizé has a gentle, repetitive style; it is simple to learn, and is often shared by huge numbers of Christian pilgrims who gather at the community. The music plays a significant part in a powerful experience for them. Compared with the intensity of feeling generated there, however, a performance of a Taizé chant in an entirely different context can be disappointing, or less impressive to anyone who has not experienced the original atmosphere and ethos. This is not to say that the music of Taizé should not be used anywhere else, but rather that when it is, those performing it should be aware that, at its best, it is part of a religious experience which includes factors other than music.

In a similar way, some music may properly belong to the large and beautiful churches, whilst other styles may be heard to best advantage within the scale, space and atmosphere of a large outdoor Christian festival, the like of which cannot necessarily be emulated in a parish church every Sunday morning.

Other Rooms and Buildings

The church itself is not the only room or building which has a bearing upon the musical possibilities. Depending upon the complexity of the musical structure, available space can vary between rehearsal rooms and vestries to a full range of teaching facilities, including a music school. These go hand in hand with whatever system has been adopted by a particular church, and they can play an essential part in the strife for excellence.

The greater the number of buildings, however, and the more specific the purpose for which they were built, the more set the structure of the music within them is likely to be, and the less open to change. Compare with the case of a simple brick garage put up to accommodate one small car. There are three brick walls, a roof and a garage door. The car is a Mini, and the garage is built to accommodate it. In time, the owner wants to change to a big estate car, but she finds it will not fit in the garage, so buys another Mini after all. By now, it is the garage which is dictating to the owner the size of the car which she can buy. The building which once *served* a purpose now *defines* the purpose for which it can be used.

Limitation need not be oppressive. To recognize what cannot be achieved within given boundaries is also to see what can. A building becomes a creative limitation when its possibilities are understood and used in a way which is true to what it is. In musical terms, this happens when its physical properties of acoustic and design are matched with music which is true to the building and to the people who inhabit it.

CHAPTER 3

Music and People

> How easily acquired is the material on which the painter and
> the sculptor body forth their ideas – a piece of canvas or a block
> of stone. The musician's material are human beings.
>
> (S. S. Wesley, *A Few Words on Cathedral Music*)

We live in an age when music is easily separated from the people
who make it. Less than a hundred years ago this could not be
done: before the days of gramophone disc and magnetic tape
every performance was live. Today, people can select music and
listen to it whenever they like.

One of the effects of this is that it is easy to forget the human
element in music. Church music, like every other kind, is about
people. Those who make music in churches, however, are grouped
together in a quite different way from those elsewhere. The City
of Barchester Chamber Orchestra (CBCO), for example, has a
national and international reputation. For its members – all of
them full-time professionals – it is their instrumental ability
which primarily determines whether they are part of the orchestra
or not. Once they have been auditioned and appointed they
become a community, but it is the level of musical ability which
comes first.

At St Mary's Barchester, on the other hand, there is no musical
requirement for anyone who joins the church. Everyone is welcome.
The community exists for reasons which are nothing to do with
music, namely, a common belief in Jesus Christ. From within the

community, a musical nucleus is found. In this sense, the CBCO and St Mary's music group are opposites. In one, music makes the community, while in the other, the community makes music.

Pastoral and Social Implications

Any musical organization within a church – be it choir or instrumental group – becomes a social unit, along with its other clubs and societies. It may have a more specific purpose and function than others, but often fewer membership requirements. A youth group, for example, may specify that its members are aged between fourteen and eighteen, or there may be one designed for the women of a church within a particular age range. A musical organization has no reason to be so specific about age or gender. Barchester Cathedral, because of its tradition and foundation, has an all-male choir, but the musical organizations of all the other churches in the town are open to people of either sex and of all ages. The choir at St Peter's Church includes boys, girls, men and women aged between six and eighty.

Music at St Peter's, therefore, is a strong unifying force. It brings together males and females of all ages before God on equal terms and with an exactly equal purpose. It has to be admitted, however, that it makes for an unusual social group, and the choir secretary has to work hard to make sure it hangs together on a personal level and continues to grow. The minister and the organist accept that not every member of every choir shares, or even understands, their ideals. People are attracted for different reasons, only some of them religious or musical. Some of the youngsters join because their friends are in the choir. Some of the adults are there because their children have joined – and vice versa. A group of the teenagers go for a drink together after choir practice and enjoy the social links.

In the period of experimentation and expansion of musical styles which has taken place over the last decade or so, this social facet of church music has suffered badly. At St Swithun's, just outside Barchester, they have introduced a range of styles performed by several different groups of musicians or soloists. They saw a growing desire in some quarters to cater for as many tastes as possible. But the musical consequence was to fragment musicians within the church, rather than unite them, because of the co-existence of several music groups. There is a small choir of elderly but committed singers who provide the music for a traditional service twice each month. There is a folk group which plays for most of the other services, and a rock band which plays once a month. Then there are other people who are called upon from time to time.

The number of people contributing to the church's music is slightly larger than it used to be when there was just a single group. Some are happy to play now and again but not every week. But the group is much less well defined than it used to be when St Swithun's choir sang for every service, and some of the people who play in different groups do not even know each other.

Furthermore, the worst side of human nature is beginning to show itself, and seems to be bringing competition. Some of the choir took umbrage recently when band practice was moved from Friday to Thursday – choir practice night. They found out only when one of their number failed to appear because he had decided to help out with the band. John and Carol, who organize the band, did not realize there was a clash or that they were 'poaching' a singer from choir practice. The competitive edge is an unwanted development at St Swithun's. It is shifting musical endeavour away from any useful purpose within the church's life, and making for an unnecessary, and sometimes ugly, distraction from its worship.

The Musicians' Material

Of all religious inheritance, music is the most difficult to maintain. The great cathedral churches of the medieval period, with their intricate carvings and sculptures, stand from one generation to the next, changing only by slow decay and repair. Music, on the other hand, is more like an enormous shape of moulded jelly being turned out onto a tray and carried around so that it wobbles in and out and from side to side. The composer makes the mould, and the ingredients of performance are poured in; but only when the jelly is turned out does the music exist, and then it cannot stand still. People interpret it. They turn their feelings into sound, and no two performances are ever the same.

When music is heard, a further variable is introduced. Music which is played and heard involves at least two human beings – the person who is playing the music and the one who is listening to it. A cellist sits down to play one of the Bach solo partitas. She has just lost a loved relative and is feeling profoundly sad. Her playing is heard by a young lad who has just passed some important exams. The music fits the cellist's state of mind well and it moves powerfully within her. But it does not connect with the young lad, who wants to hear something fast, loud and rhythmic. He finds the cello music dreary. Some time later, the positions are reversed: when she plays the piece again, she finds herself in a peaceful and joyful frame of mind. The young lad – now not quite so young – is searching unsuccessfully for a job and feeling rather less elated than he had been before. Everything has changed. The way the music is played is different, and so is the way it is heard. So, the music itself has changed. The mould is the same, but the jelly has twisted into another shape.

An Element of Sacrifice

Because music is brought about by organizing people, it follows that the performance of church music has an inbuilt element of sacrifice. As the most extreme example, take the music of a working monastery whose *opus Dei* (God's work) is the recitation of the offices of the day, sung to plainsong. From the point of view of an occasional visitor, what is heard may create the sensation of deep, timeless spirituality, and it may be a moving religious experience.

42

But in order for that to exist, a number of human beings have given over their whole life to a system of religious observance. The music which results from it, therefore, is the product of sacrifice in human terms. Whatever privilege or enjoyment is derived from that way of life, the wholesale commitment of human life is essential.

None of the churches in Barchester demands that degree of sacrifice, and probably none of them ever will. Nevertheless, in order for music to be produced in any systematic way, the individuals concerned must abide by the system and sacrifice time in order to fulfil their commitment to it. In theory, a perfect match is in the offing. Music is performed at its best when it is the product of systematic preparation. Religion is a systematic expression of spiritual concepts. People and system are common to both.

Opportunities and Limitations

Predictability, order and structure lend themselves well to the practicalities of making music. On 25 December 2996, for example, Christians all over the world will be celebrating Christmas Day. We could start planning now.

But they also limit. Once you have entered a system, that part of your person which does not fit into it is necessarily excluded. It is no good a footballer lamenting the fact that he has no opportunity to show his prowess with a cricket bat. If he wishes to play football *and* cricket, he may do so, but not at the same time. Each sport uses a different set of rules. Neither claims to be the complete and definitive' one. We know that each is only one game and a part of the whole sporting world.

Christians spend a good deal of time looking over their shoulders to see what others are achieving and what they themselves are not. No doubt aware of the omnipotent nature of God, and of his infinite manifestations, Christians are inclined to be wary of any activity which ties them into too small a part of his totality. There is a feeling, consequently, that a performance of a piece of music such as a sixteenth-century motet may appear too small an achievement to which to devote a given part of your life. A series of rehearsals stretching over a period of weeks may seem too great a sacrifice of time and energy to expend on such a finite end. To return to the monastery, there is a feeling that the singing of chants at certain hours of the day represents too small a part of God's creation to demand such a significant sacrifice of the human life.

Such arguments, though sincerely held, confuse faith and religion. Religion is limited in a way which faith is not. There is no case to be argued that any liturgy represents a complete expression of God in words. No one would argue that a text embellished with the music of a sixteenth-century motet fully shows the divine nature of God in music. It represents only a tiny part of it. Its performance achieves something which has boundaries and which can therefore be achieved through human endeavour. But by attaining that which *can* be attained through human endeavour, the way is left open to receive what cannot, which comes only by the grace of God. It is said that you can put God into the *whole* of life only by first putting him into very specific parts of it. In the same way can you do everything for God only by first doing specific things for him. The performance of a piece of music, well chosen and well rehearsed, is one such thing. It is no more, but it is certainly no less.

Inspiration and Perspiration

The fact that music is so dependent upon humanity for its existence has a bearing upon the quality of music which is suited to religious worship. Human emotion and feeling cannot be entirely separated from the spirit inherent in the music, and the two aspects interact and feed each other. In other words, the music can have an effect on human feeling, just as human feeling can have an effect on the music. Music which is performed as part of

44

a religion, therefore, plays a part in shaping the spirituality of those who perform it.

An actress once told me about the effect the parts she played had upon her own character. 'You try to approach them purely as professional engagements,' she said, 'but they do begin to seep into you. There are some parts I will not play.' Fine art dealers talk of a spiritual dimension which comes from spending their lives handling beautiful things, not only because they are beautiful in themselves, but also because they seem to cross the boundaries of normal human achievement. It is a feeling which is not shared by someone who sells kitchen utensils. Asked to choose between a Fabergé egg and a plastic container, there is no doubt which is the more practical for storing a spoonful of leftover beans. But the Fabergé egg offers something else. It represents that which is normally unattainable, and which creates a spirit of wonder and awe.

Some church musicians deal in Fabergé eggs, others in plastic bowls. Some have to deal with both. A piece of music such as Allegri's *Miserere* contains that numinous quality which is inimitable. It is a quality which goes beyond normal technique and analysis and into a world of divine inspiration. It is as though the music had been discovered, or even revealed, rather than composed. Something of its mystery rubs off every time it is performed, and the people who perform it are left covered in a thin coat of divine creation. With repetition, the coat becomes a little thicker.

Music which is functional or for every day also makes its mark. Because in church services the music is the servant of the liturgy, it is sometimes argued that the character of the music should be primarily functional rather than inspirational in its own right. To some degree, this argument holds good, but only up to a point. It would certainly be easier to stick with if the music could do without people. It is easier to imagine the circumstance of a church musician commenting on a piece which has been sung in the course of a service saying, 'That piece was wonderful: I began

45

to glimpse the Divine,' than it would be to imagine the same person saying, 'What a magnificent piece: it seemed so functional.' There is a dulling of the spirit which comes from constant exposure to the second rate.

Reaching for the Moon

The human tendency is to strive for that which is beyond them. People sometimes ask why it is that humankind can walk on the moon but cannot solve the problems of homelessness or famine, which, on the face of it, are more easily solved. Part of this is to do with inspiration. People are inspired by the things which are beyond and above them, and bored by those things which lie within their means and control. It is a standard principle of management in any business that employees, if they are to give of their best, must be stretched, or inspired to achieve slightly more than they think they can.

People thrive upon encouragement and praise. This can only be done sincerely when there is something good to praise. Though in itself this may not be a reason to decide upon a musical style, it is part of a total picture which has at the centre of its understanding not a remote ideology or theory of sound but a recognition that it is people that turn sound into music, and ultimately, therefore, that people come first.

CHAPTER 4

The Plan

There are three months before Christmas. At Barchester Cathedral, term has just begun. Simon Morgan, the organist, has spent the summer planning, and everything is in place until Christmas Day. The Dean has asked the choir to learn three new pieces for three special diocesan carol services. Mr Morgan knows that December will be a very busy time. He is not unduly worried, however, since he will see his choir every day between now and then, and has the time he needs, so long as he plans it carefully. In November, he has chosen pieces which most of the choir already knows, and he has made sure that some of the Sunday music in November will already have been sung on a weekday in October. This releases a little extra rehearsal time in the month before Christmas to get ahead before the festive season. The extra burden can be met with no additional rehearsal.

At St Mary's, they have a problem. The Rector has asked for a communion motet to be sung once a month. This is an awkward request, because there is no choir. The music in the church is led by an instrumental group and up to half a dozen singers who do not sing in parts. The Rector points out, however, that he is used to a communion motet from his previous church (where there was a good choir) and he feels it enhanced the power of the service. So, each month, Mrs Smith rings round some of her friends to see whether there are enough people to sing a motet in four parts. It is uphill work, and she spends literally hours on the telephone. Three people would be happy in principle, but cannot make the

Friday rehearsal. She decides to try Thursday instead, and telephones the four people who had agreed to Friday. Two of them cannot make Thursday. She eventually finds eight people, and borrows some music from St Peter's for them to sing. In the end, three of the singers cancel at the last moment, and the motet is abandoned with the promise to try again next month.

The essential difference here is between a musical system which ties in with the religious system, and one which does not. The religious system at St Mary's demands a monthly motet, but the musical one does not provide for it. Without it, even the simplest of requests becomes prohibitively difficult.

The people at St Mary's, like those of all the other churches, now have to make a plan. To do so, they need to know what the music is for, what the possibilities and limitations of the building are, and which people are available to perform the music they have chosen. Next they must find a way to pull these strands together to serve their regular pattern of worship.

In recent years, Christians have developed a fear, or at least a suspicion, of system and order. There is a feeling that a service of worship which has been planned six months in advance, and which is supported by planning and rehearsal, is to deny the influence of the Holy Spirit. There is a fear also that the framework may become of overriding importance, so that the religion, far from nourishing a faith, distances the believer from it.

Yet in other fields of human activity, people recognize the value of order as a means to an end. A group of lads may enjoy kicking a football round a park, but the game only becomes an engaging and exciting spectator sport when it is played according to certain rules. It achieves further popularity with the introduction of skill, which is also learnt in a systematic way in training and practice. The measurements of the pitch and the limitations of the movements which are permitted, then, form the backbone to the structure, while the arrangements for training, teaching and practice complete it. When the match is played, it is then that the creative spirit of the players is released, as they strive to achieve what they can within the set limits of the game.

In the same way, if music is to be performed on a regular basis, inside or outside the church, a good system and structure is always needed. This is a musical rather than religious requirement, but unless it is met, the music will not serve the religious purposes for which it was introduced.

Music is added to a service of worship because it possesses certain qualities which will enhance it in some deliberate way. A polyphonic anthem is included as a sacrificial offering to God; a Taizé chant is included for its meditative quality and because it involves the entire congregation; a modern rock song because of its exuberance. But the music will possess those qualities only if it is performed as it should be, and for that to happen, the appropriate ingredients have to be assembled in a certain way. If they are not, things go badly wrong.

A policy decision is taken by a minister, for example, to introduce a modern style of folk music in order to attract young people to the church. Once the decision has been made, the instruments must be found and parts written out for them, so that they have something to play. If this is not done, the sounds will not be at all attractive, and the music's power to appeal to the people for whom it was intended will disappear.

Alternatively, a policy decision is taken by a minister to introduce polyphonic choral music to bring a numinous quality to the church's worship. That happens, however, only when the music is performed to a certain standard. In order to achieve it, the singers must rehearse and be trained, and an appropriate schedule set in place for this; if it is not, then the music never reaches the point at which its ethereal quality emerges.

Much of this comes down to the fact that it is easier to articulate words *about* music than it is to achieve results *through* music. But unless these are attained, there is little point in the rhetoric.

Something for Everybody?

The most difficult policy to fulfil is the 'catholic taste' policy that they have gone for at St Mary's. The minister knows his congregation, and he knows it is diverse. There is a lorry driver, a school teacher, a marine biologist, a professional runner and a school leaver who all sit together in the same pew. He is keen to include something for everyone, old and new, an anthem, a pop song, a folk chorus and a rousing hymn. This is the perfect example of how much simpler it is to speak policy than it is to practise it: 'We need music to cater for all tastes,' he says. The comment slips easily off the tongue, but it sets a goal which is impossible for any but the best-resourced and most intricately-structured church to achieve or come anywhere near achieving. Indeed it requires a solution which has so far eluded the whole of the commercial world which has a vested interest in discovering that elusive musical genre or mix which genuinely caters for every taste.

This is the point at which a musical constitution acquires a religious significance, and at which policy and practice must be taken together. Which takes the greater influence, however, is another matter. Do the terms of the foundation of a well-established choir guarantee the continued use of choral music, or does the decision to have a choir come first and the framework develop accordingly, to make it possible?

In the first place, it would usually be the decision about the type of music which comes first, and the structure which then emerges. Once it is set, however, a structure begins to dictate further decisions, and to influence the subsequent development of musical life within a church. In some cases, the initial decision was taken by an earlier society or era, as is the case with many of the English cathedral choral foundations. Since then, provision has been built up through legacies, scholarships, educational institutions and the like, to maintain them. To subsequent generations, these seem to have more influence on policy than the people who now work and live within the cathedrals.

The age of a musical structure, however, has nothing to do with the age of the music within it. It is perfectly possible (and normal) for a choir founded four hundred years ago to perform a piece of music written yesterday. What was decided all those centuries ago is the resources that are available to perform music, the type of timetable by which singers rehearse and perform, and how the musical system is made to work with other factors in their lives, such as employment and education. But these past generations did not decide what music would be sung. The system, in other words, is an enabling force, which allows for the performance of a repertory of music known at the time of its foundation. This repertory can then be expanded, provided the basic genre remains constant.

For example, there is a collection of choral music for four voices. A system is set up to perform it. Once it is in place the repertory may be expanded infinitely, provided it stays within the bounds of choral music for four voices. If the need is to expand to solo song with instrumental backing, this cannot be done within the existing system.

The Germans showed in the seventeenth and eighteenth centuries that successful ways could be found to organize instrumentalists in just the same way, and there is no doubt that there are means by which any style of music, be it folk or rock, may be regularly performed. The greater the number of styles and combinations of musicians that are required, the more complex the system will be.

Don't Play It Again

Some types of music, however, lend themselves better to ordered performance and religious observance than others. Some is written to be used and quickly thrown away. Ephemeral music is that which everyone, including the composer, agrees is not intrinsically great, but which has some other merit, such as simplicity, so that it can be very quickly learned. A performance of such a piece sung by a large gathering can create a strong community feeling.

This is the sort of bond which you sometimes experience when travelling in a foreign country in which the language used is very unfamiliar. While struggling to communicate, you hit on a few words which, along with other gestures and expressions, seem to get through and make some sense. Though the words may be ungrammatically linked and even incorrect, they acquire some significance at that moment because they have been a vehicle for communication. In that circumstance the sense of bond between the two people is often quite out of proportion to the substance of what they have said to one another, because they have a common experience of having overcome a barrier.

On the other hand, the words which are used at that moment are unlikely to be revered as great literature, written down for subsequent use and repetition, or even remembered by either party. They have served their purpose and will be forgotten. This type of moment is quite common in personal relationships, where trivial events acquire a significance through shared experience. Two friends reminisce, 'Do you remember the time when you fell into the river?' They go over what happened in lurid detail and laugh at the absurdity of it all. Now try the same story on someone who was not there and who knows neither person. 'They were playing a ball game, someone threw the ball too far, and he stepped backwards into the river.' Without the intimacy and shared experience, the story falls flat.

In building a religion, we seek components which possess the opposite attributes. We seek words which can be passed to another, and used by the receiver in the same way that they were used by the giver. We seek words, therefore, which are beautiful or meaningful or uplifting in their own right, and not merely because of a secondary association. If we do not, we are liable to generate a sequence of exclusive and unrelated spiritual experiences separated by periods of time, rather than a continuous religion incorporating the divine revelation given to people of previous generations.

52

Lagging Behind

Religion sits uncomfortably with a desire to keep up with the times. In the commercial world, musical taste is constantly changing. In the world of popular music, for example, the top ten hits change weekly, as different groups and styles lurch in and out of the bounds of widespread public approval. To keep up with the times is to move fast. It will not do to know what was all the rage ten years ago, one year ago or even one month ago. It is the scene today which counts. Religion, on the other hand, works slowly, and its music is no exception. Tunes are tried here, retried there. Books are printed, published and slowly distributed. Congregations have a go, and some of the tunes catch on. Eventually, they become standard repertoire for a while. Some of them are oversung and die an early death, while others hang on to find their way into the weighty hymn- or song-book next time it is revised. Some of the 'modern' tunes of today are ten years or more old. Graham Kendrick's 'The Servant King', for example, was written in 1983. Who can remember what hit the charts that year?

The reason for the disparity is not difficult to find. When a hit single is released it makes its impact through the instant media of radio and television broadcasting. The song will have been recorded by star performers, with top-grade professionals as backing, in high-quality – and very expensive – studio conditions. By the time the track is released, every detail and nuance of the performance has been finalized, and the track is ready to be replayed. But that is all. It is not designed for reperformance in a thousand different ways. No one has to rescore it, learn it and then teach it to a disparate gathering of individuals of different ages and from different cultural backgrounds and traditions.

The very latest music can certainly be heard and performed in church, but it cannot immediately be used in a corporate way as part of its religion. The Church, and religion, need time.

A Switch in Style

The advent of electronic music and the use of electronics in music is the most radical development in church music there has ever been. It is something of which those who established musical foundations before this century knew nothing and could not have taken into account, and in this respect the present difficulties in church music are historically unique. The extent of divergence between available styles is new, both aesthetically from the point of view of the listener, and practically from that of the performer. So while there have always been differences between working with singers and with instrumentalists, for example, or between the music of the Church and that of the entertainment world, none of the ranges of difference has ever been so great as they are today.

A Square Peg in a Round Hole

Perhaps for the first time, the range of available styles has pushed musical structures beyond the limits of compatibility. Think how the carol has been moulded over the years. In medieval times, the carol was a musical accompaniment to dance inside or outside a church. It belongs to a popular folk style, with simple words which are easily learned and remembered. The music itself is not of a high spiritual order, but it is tuneful, rhythmic, harmonically simple and has a 'catchy' quality to it. Take the tune of the carol 'The Holly and the Ivy' as an example, which may be harmonized in the way shown on the page opposite. It is easy to imagine how this arrangement might sound if sung outside by a dozen people as they step to a simple dance, accompanied by a couple of guitars and a bit of percussion (a drum or tambourine), or the people clapping as they sing. Performed in this way, the music has a certain rustic quality about it, which matches the words well.

Example 1. 'The Holly and the Ivy': folk-style arrangement

As a contrast, the same music, reharmonized by Henry Walford Davies, gives a rather different effect. A few bars are printed overleaf. In comparison with the first arrangement, the music is much more sophisticated. It has been rewritten to suit a different musical genre, that of the four-part choir. In so doing, Walford Davies has drawn upon the tradition of choral music, and superimposed it upon the original melody. The sound of this arrangement, sung in a large resonant building by the trained voices of a disciplined choir, will contrast dramatically with that of the first example. Placed in an atmosphere of dim candlelight, its whole effect will be entirely different again.

It is tempting to think that the second arrangement has been made to alter the style, and give to the music a different character

Example 2. 'The Holly and the Ivy': arranged by Henry Walford Davies

which is more suitable for use in church. What has happened in this example, though, is that the music has been adapted to suit not only a style, but an ecclesiastical structure. Because a foundation supports a four-part choir, it is important that the choral arrangement is in four parts, and that the writing of the inner parts is vocal in style.

Over a period of time, then, music and structure begin to interact and influence each other. A structure is set up in the first instance to perform a particular repertory of music, but once it is in place, other music is adapted to suit it, so that an intricate polyphonic motet and a simple dance-carol come within the scope of the same group of performers, and within the same system of rehearsal and performance practice. The music may be compromised as this happens, as different styles are pushed together into a common mould. As they diversify, however, the degree of compromise reaches a point where uniformity is too great a price to pay.

Cathedral Rock

Let us consider, for example, the case of a cathedral choir, with organ, performing a song written originally with a rock band backing in mind.

It begins with an introduction based on sustained chords such as these, played on a gentle, 'stringy' synthesizer sound:

Example 3. Synthesizer chords

Over these, other electronic effects are added. First, some descending, 'breathy' pitched sounds, panning from right to left in the stereo sound mix. Next come some quiet marimba-type sounds scattered across the picture, a little percussion sound (cymbals), and another chord. Then comes a solo singer, or 'vocal', using a microphone fed into a sound sampling system which changes the timbre of the voice, amplifies the sound and places it into an echo chamber. One line is sung, in an intimate, almost whispered, manner, before the music changes character completely: at this point, the main battery of percussion sounds is introduced in a heavy, rhythmic sequence, and the tempo moves upbeat. The next part brings in a question-and-answer idea between the principal vocalist and a small backing group of four singers.

In performance, the music is played on two keyboards, one for the chords, and the other for the pre-recorded backing tracks with the breathy sounds and marimba. Some of the percussion is generated from the synthesizers, while part is played by a drummer. There is also an electric guitar to give solid support to the harmonic sequence. In addition, the style of the music is complemented by other means of presentation: lighting is chosen to add colour and variety to the performance, and some physical movement on the singers' part adds vitality and extra spectacle.

Now consider the same piece of music performed by a cathedral choir with organ in the course of a cathedral service. Taking the music in sequence: it begins with sustained chords, presumably played on the organ, using a 'string' stop. The descending effects, marimbas and percussion are replaced by other sounds in order to avoid the chords becoming over-long. It may be possible to add solo sounds from the organ, or rhythmized versions of the chords sung by the choir. The vocal part is performed either by a soloist or by a semi-chorus, though in the context of a cathedral service, the timbre of the voice cannot be processed, and the result is a 'straight' or 'natural' performance. At the point at which the character of the music changes, it has to be modified much more. The question-and-answer effect works well between the semi-chorus and the choir, but the lack of percussion which underpinned the whole rhythmic thrust of the rock version is badly missed, leaving the choir parts seeming unnecessarily slow and a little lifeless. This is compensated for, therefore, by the addition of a virtuoso organ part with the left hand playing mainly rapid semiquaver passages, while the right hand and pedal parts play the chord sequence. The additional effects of performance are omitted, since variations in lighting are not possible and loose movement does not lend itself either to choir-stalls or to a surpliced choir.

Rock Group Goes Choral

Now let us consider the reverse case, of the same group of rock musicians performing an anthem. Since we have quoted his words, let us take a piece by S. S. Wesley: 'Blessed be the God and Father'. (See Appendix B.) The opening section in the original is scored for unaccompanied four-part choir. Assuming that the backing group happened to be all women, it might be most effective to leave the opening section to the lead vocalist with a light synthesizer accompaniment, without percussion. The melody may need to be adjusted at one point in order to avoid a top treble G, depending upon the range of the vocalist. The next section is originally written for full tenors and basses, but could still be sung as a melody line by the lead vocalist. The change of scoring would need to be represented in a different way, perhaps by introducing different sounds on the synthesizer, and adding a light rhythmic percussion. For the section, 'Love one another', in comes the backing group for the antiphonal effect, with light cymbals in place of the semiquaver movement. The full works are saved for the climactic section, 'But the word of the Lord', which can be rescored for singer, vocal backing and the full band, including bass guitar. The fugue at the end will be more difficult to represent, and will need to be rewritten. To the rescoring is added some imaginative lighting with something dramatic for 'But the word of the Lord', and the effect is complete.

Possible though it may be to rework the music in each direction, the end result is likely to prove disastrous, especially to those who know either piece in its original form. It is also questionable whether the amount of time taken to adapt the music has been well spent, given the built-in difficulties, when it could be used preparing music which is more ideally suited to the available musicians. Thirdly, if this reworking is done with the purpose of satisfying all tastes, it will almost certainly fail, and satisfy none.

This example takes the extreme case in order to represent one aspect of a decision which has to be made every time a mix of styles and cultures is matched, or mismatched, with a different combination of structure, resource and tradition. Between the two extremes, there are varying degrees of mismatch.

A Match Made on Earth

If a piece of music has been requested which does not immediately suit the musical structure of the church, a number of options are available.

One is to reject it. This may be simply on the grounds that it is a mismatch, or it may take into account other factors, such as the building's reverberance, or lack of it.

The second option is to change the way the performers are organized to suit the music. It will be a total change if, say, the system is designed to support the existence of a four-part choir, but the policy in the church is to promote the use of rock music only. The four-part choir is then permanently disbanded and an entirely new structure set in place. A partial change comes about if the use of the rock music is less extensive. The extent of the change depends upon the balance between the two styles. In altering the structure, however, it is necessary to assess whether it will be damaged or strengthened, and in particular whether its present purpose is compromised.

In this case, the third option may be preferred, which is to keep the existing set-up intact, but to add to it a new superstructure which runs concurrently. Suppose now that a new weekly service is introduced, offering a different style of music, while retaining all features of existing services. In our example, the four-part choir is supported as before and has the same purpose as before, but, in addition, there is a rock group within the same church and church building. At first sight this often appears to be the most attractive solution in that it appears to satisfy elements of conservatism and innovation. In practice, however, it can create its own difficulties because it tends to cause fragmentation or, worse, schism, and introduces an element of competition, not only between the two results, but between the two structures. This may involve use of rehearsal rooms, financial resources or particular buildings or facilities.

The fourth option is to change the music to suit the structure in the way which has already been described.

The last three of these all represent change in the way things are organized. The extent to which this may be accommodated depends upon the efficiency of the existing framework. In general, the more efficient it is, the more specific it will be to a particular purpose, and the less easy it is to break into.

Founded of Old

The cathedral choir in Barchester was founded in 1396, the year in which its vicars choral became a collegiate body. The college buildings are still inhabited. After the Reformation, Queen Elizabeth's statutes ordained that the musical establishment was to consist of twelve vicars choral and eight choristers, making certain provisions for them, funded partly by rent from adjoining land. The statutes still hold good, and the Barchester boys delight in the official distinction between the eight choristers and the ten 'singing boys' who were later added to the foundation. It is, by several hundred years, the oldest musical structure in Barchester. In its six-hundred-year history it has had its high and low points, but it has survived the most enormous changes, the break with Rome and rebuilding of the cathedral to name but two.

The cathedral choir is made up of a treble line of boys who are educated at the cathedral's own choir school. The boys, when they audition for the choir, are usually about eight years old, so they are chosen for their potential ability to learn and sing rather than for any particular skills already acquired.

The alto, tenor and bass members of the choir are now called the 'lay clerks', and they are all male. The altos sing in a *falsetto* voice known as counter-tenor, with a range which is slightly lower than that of the female alto. The lay clerks at Barchester are all semi-professional singers, with good voices and sight-reading ability. The rehearsal pattern of the choir is not laid down by ancient statute. The timetable was chosen by the last Master of the Choristers but one and the headmaster of the school at the time, but it follows a long established tradition:

Rehearsal timetable, Barchester Cathedral Choir

	morning (before school)	afternoon	later afternoon
Monday	boys' rehearsal	full rehearsal	Evensong
Tuesday	boys' rehearsal	full rehearsal	Evensong
Thursday	boys' rehearsal	full rehearsal	Evensong
Friday	boys' rehearsal	men's rehearsal	Evensong (men's voices only)
Saturday	boys' rehearsal	full rehearsal	Evensong
Sunday	full rehearsal followed by Matins/Eucharist	full rehearsal	Evensong

They maintain this pattern in order to prepare the music for the daily singing of Choral Evensong. The boys have a rehearsal before school begins, so that they can be taught the music for Evensong by the Master of the Choristers or his assistant. The morning rehearsal gives an opportunity for vocal exercises and training, and the development of general skills such as the ability to sight-read. The music has been planned so that a certain amount of the repertoire will be familiar to some of the boys, and in this way the youngsters learn from older choristers who have sung it before. The morning rehearsals are not always limited to the music for that day's service. Time is spent on pieces to be sung later in the week, especially if there is anything difficult or new.

The lay clerks either will know the music, or will have learnt it in advance of the full rehearsal, which is spent putting the parts together, and adding the finer musical points to the performance. Evensong is then sung after a short break for refreshment and robing. When a lay clerk has to be away for a service it is up to him to find an approved deputy, so that the number of singers at any service is always the same.

At Barchester, there is no choir commitment on Wednesdays, giving all members a rest from the usual pattern. On Friday, the service is sung by the lay clerks only, so that the boys' rehearsal that morning may be used to prepare for the weekend's music, which is often more demanding than that sung during the remainder of the week. In particular, they may learn pieces for Sunday at this rehearsal, since there is no time for a boys' practice that day.

Even with such a full rehearsal pattern, they find there is not the time to rehearse every note of every service even once. The system works, then, only on the basis of regularity and continuity, and on the understanding that a certain proportion of the music in any term will be known to some of the choir from previous terms.

The essential point about the pattern is that, by sticking strictly to it, and by careful planning on the part of the Master of the Choristers, a huge quantity of music, some of it technically difficult, is sung to a high standard in the course of a year.

The schedule at Barchester Cathedral is not kept going for its own sake, or as a way of preserving heritage or upholding tradition. Its value is that it enables music to be sung well in a particular style of Christian worship. The Dean and the Headmaster agree that it would not be possible to maintain the standard or repertoire of choral music without a similarly structured timetable of rehearsal and performance or without the continuity which that provides. They also know that without it, a large proportion of sacred music would fall out of the reach of church music. These days, most of the polyphonic repertoire, for example, lies outside the scope of the neighbouring church choirs which have done away with the support structures which once enabled the more complex styles of music to be sung.

Springing from the Roots

From the middle of the last century until a few years ago, the cathedral choir was the model to which St Mary's, St Peter's and all the other parish church choirs aspired. This is no longer the case. For one thing, at the cathedral the 1662 Prayer Book is still used at Evensong every day. None of the parish churches in Barchester uses the old service for Evensong any longer (except once a month at St Peter's).

Even in the early period, of course, there were differences. Choir members would be amateur singers who were part of the church congregation and services would normally be limited to Sundays and other special days. The alto line would more often be provided by women than men, and the treble line often comprised a mixture of sopranos and children. At St Mary's, they used to have daily rehearsals for various sections of the choir. (The boys came in three times a week, the men once, and there were two full rehearsals.) Even at St Swithun's, choir members were committed to a weekly practice and two Sunday services. Suddenly, the model which had served the cathedral for so many hundreds of years ceased to be the blueprint any longer.

At St Peter's, on the other hand, the parish choir is still greatly valued in the musical life of a church. Of all its organizations, it is the most inclusive, accommodating an almost unlimited membership of all ages and both sexes. The weekly rehearsal time is divided into two, starting with the younger members and joining forces with the older members for the second part of the rehearsal. This comes from the idea down at the cathedral, of the choristers' morning rehearsal, at which notes are learned and at which some attention is paid to vocal technique and to other singing skills.

The type of music in the repertoire will attract or put off certain people. Likewise, the choir members will influence what music is possible. It is not always easy to decide which factor should come first, and perhaps not important, so long as they match.

As a simple analogy, it is no use running a football team and then asking the team members to switch to tennis. If you want tennis players, they have to be trained and coached in a different way. If, on the other hand, you already have an accomplished football team, you might do well to think twice before deciding that tennis is the better option for them.

Looking back, they now know that this is something which went wrong at St Mary's. The minister at the time wanted mostly folk and pop styles, which he had heard used to good effect in other churches. They were written to be sung in unison rather than in parts, however, and they left the four-part choir at St Mary's with nothing to do. The musical set-up was not changed to accommodate such a major switch in policy, and was left to fall apart.

Moving to Another Era

The door opens at St Mary's Rectory and in comes Rebecca Mortone. The rest of the worship committee at St Mary's have already arrived and they are delighted to see their new director of music. This is the first time they will have talked about music properly since the choir was disbanded with such acrimony all that time ago. Officially, Rebecca starts in her post next week, but she has already been thinking hard about what should be done. 'Whatever we do,' the Rector tells them, 'the starting point is where we are now. This church cannot cope with another clean start. I have appointed Rebecca on a half-time salary, because I want her to take things in hand.'

At the moment they have five instrumentalists and a few singers. 'I noticed Harry Viddler in the congregation the other week,' observes Rebecca. 'He plays in the CBCO. Why doesn't he play here?' No one had ever dared ask him. With the music at its lowest ebb for years, they had naturally assumed he would want no part of it. 'If we can get things going, I would hope that people like him will join in. He would be a tremendous help for the others.' Rebecca has already talked through her ideas with the Rector. Now she has the floor for the whole of the worship committee.

'I am happy with the idea of having instruments,' Rebecca begins. 'The church has all those big wooden pews which soak up a lot of sound and leave it without much reverberance.' Meaningful looks pass among them. How they had wanted to get rid of the pews! 'I think it has the right acoustic for instrumental players, but they cannot squeeze in between the choir-stalls. We will have to find somewhere else. The next thing is that we need instrumental parts. At the moment, there is nothing to play. I cannot imagine how they have managed all these years.' Everyone looks down for a moment. The truth is they have not managed very well. 'I reckon it will take me about one day to compose and write out a set of parts for each piece we do. I cannot spend more than two days each week writing arrangements, so at first we will have to limit ourselves to two pieces with instruments for each service. In time, once there is a library of parts, this can be increased. Now, talking of that, I'm worried by the amount of paper there will be flying around. Orchestral parts have a tendency to walk away. People take them away to practise and they forget to bring them back. I should like to be able to store the parts on computer and print out copies only when they are needed. It also means that they can be adapted for other instruments much more easily, so that when someone leaves or joins, I don't necessarily have to start again.' Everything sounds good so far.

'The next thing is to build up the choir.' This does not sound so good. The thought of returning to those days is not to be entertained. 'We don't have a choir,' someone says. 'Yes we do,' says Rebecca, 'there are half a dozen singers who help with the songs. Call them a singing group if you like. And there must be more people who could be encouraged to join from a congregation this size. They also need parts to sing and time to learn them. Besides, the Rector has asked for a monthly communion motet, and that needs to be worked into the system too. To begin with, I suggest that each service works on a two-week cycle:

Proposed timetable for St Mary's Barchester

Day 1/2	Sat/Sun	Music secretary finds availability of players and prepares list for Day 16
Day 4	Tuesday evening	Worship committee meets to choose music
Day 6/7	Thurs/Fri	Rebecca to write parts
Day 9	Sunday	Distribute parts to be learned before rehearsal
Day 12	Wednesday 8.00–9.00 pm	Singers' practice
Day 13	Thursday 8.00–9.00 pm	Instrumental practice
Day 15	Saturday 9.00–10.00 am	Full rehearsal
Day 16	Sunday 9.30–10.00 am	Final run-through before service

'Nobody has to commit themselves to more than one weekday evening for one hour, plus one hour on Saturday morning. Although it is a two-week cycle, most people will see it as a weekly one: they get given the music on Sunday for the following week, so there is no confusion about which piece is to be sung or when.'

Things are looking up for St Mary's. There is no guarantee that the system will work. The people of St Mary's have to throw themselves into it, because without them the system will do no good. But if they take up the challenge, there is every chance that things will go well.

At What Cost?

The changes are not without a price. Rebecca is paid a half-time salary. She needs every moment of that time – a full three days each week – to compose and write out parts and prepare and take rehearsals, not to mention putting in an hour or two's organ practice herself. She is out most evenings, and a good part of the weekend is spent at church. She is helped by the PCC's acquisition of a computer system to print out music, but this has been an expensive item off the annual budget. If the repertoire is to be kept alive, new books and music have to be bought. There are copyright fees to be paid where music is copied.

Music is expensive and time-consuming. The more music you try to do, the more it costs. It is just the same for the CBCO, whose annual budget needs to be seen to be believed. They balance the books with subsidy, sponsorship and ticket sales. St Mary's has none of these.

What Has Changed?

St Mary's is not reinstating its choir, or putting things back as they were before. But they are putting system and order back into the musical life of the church, which is what they had so badly lacked.

However much people wish that structures were not important, and however much they can limit, it remains a fact that they are what convert theory and philosophy into reality. There is never anything to be gained from hoping that things will 'be OK' when the basic musical needs have not been met. It is senseless, for example, to expect that inspiration will come to musicians on the spot who have been asked to 'busk' a part because one has not been provided.

Building for God

When an architect designs a building, he draws a plan. He has to know how many pillars will hold up a roof. If he does not have enough of them, it will fall down. So he makes calculations. He does not just think of a number and hope for the best.

Before the building starts, the cost is worked out too. If it cannot be paid for, it does not go up. No one says, 'We cannot afford steel girders, so let us make do with wooden dowling.' They know the building will not stand.

Churches and cathedrals are not exempt from the basic rules. If they are not built well, they fall like any other building. Nor are they exempt from the basic system and structure which makes music work. Choices have to be made which are supportable. If they are not, they have to be rethought. Not every plan produces a beautiful building, but every beautiful building comes from a plan. Yet structure and system are not a *substitute* for spirit and artistry. Music is the huge tapestry which hangs from an iron frame. If the frame gives in, the tapestry crumples and cannot be seen. It is still there, and when the frame is repaired, it hangs again and can be seen in all its glory once again. God's way is to transform chaos into order. When order is replaced by chaos, then music no longer does glory to him who first created it.

PART II

Which Music?

---

*This section describes some of the practical and technical
details of choral and instrumental music in greater detail.*

CHAPTER 5

Choirs and Singers

The two boys skid round the corner and head for the archway which leads into the precinct of Barchester Cathedral. Everywhere they go, their precious voices go too. They slosh them round with fizzy drinks and wear them out as they yell across the football pitch. Yet everything depends on them: their school life, their education, even their religion. The practice room is right over on the other side, and they dare not cut across the grass. Although they are already late, they are trying hard not to run. If they arrive out of breath, their valuable instruments will not work.

The human voice is the oldest musical instrument, and one which has been employed for the worship of God for as long as history records. There is an intimate quality about it because it is a physical part of the human being, and because no external mechanics stand between the person and the music. Although there are technical skills which apply to vocalists as much as to instrumentalists, singing is an art which can sometimes be begun and quickly learned by those who have had no previous training. Every now and then, beautiful voices emerge which have received no formal tuition but which are the product of a natural gift.

Why Sing at All?

The human voice is the most universal instrument. In addition, it has many practical advantages which make it especially suitable for religious use: it is easy to carry around and takes up no space. It is ideal for procession and lends itself to ceremony.

Singing is the only means of combining the usual elements of music – pitch, rhythm and so on – with the articulation of words. Only by the inclusion of the human voice, therefore, can music ever be definitively sacred. Certainly, some purely instrumental items, such as organ chorale preludes, are regarded as religious because of their allusion to melodies associated with particular texts, but even then this comes about only because of an association with words. Instrumental or wordless music may evoke a mood which relates it to a form of spirituality, but not in a reliable or consistent way. Play a piece of orchestral music to two friends, and ask them what they hear. 'It is the Norfolk Broads on a cold misty morning,' says one. 'It sounds menacing to me,' says the other, 'like the calm before the storm.' Music sparks off associations and activates the imagination.

All these factors contribute to the dominance of song and choral singing in churches. There has been positive discrimination towards that which can with certainty call itself sacred. However great their impact, and however great their ability to enhance, instruments will never do more than play a supporting role to the human voice.

Can You Hear at the Back?

The sung voice is louder and therefore more audible than the spoken voice. Ask an ordinary, untrained speaker to read a poem in a large church. The people halfway down cannot hear, so he raises his voice and tries again. But still the people at the back cannot hear. By now, he has had to raise the volume of his voice so much that its natural sound starts to distort. It begins to sound like a shout. The subtle nuances of speech which the poem demands have become impossible. The speaker is confronted with a balance between audibility and intelligibility: in order for the words to be heard at all, they need to be spoken in such a way that they lose their meaning.

When you drive away in a car, you begin in first gear. If you stay in first gear for too long, the engine begins to strain and become uncomfortable. While straining, you are still not able to reach the speed you want to reach. You change gear. So does the orator in church. Ask him now to take a comfortable pitch and sing the poem on a single note. By singing, rather than speaking, his voice moves a greater amount of air in the building. The sound waves are stronger, and the people at the back can hear better, without his straining the limits of the spoken voice. So far, we are in second gear. The audibility is much better now, but the meaning of the words suffers, because everything is sung on a monotone. It is time to return to the spoken text for a while, and to make a note of the way the spoken pitch rises and falls, and which words are emphasized more than others. He looks at the text: 'The wind rustles through the trees.' The word 'rustles' is pitched a little higher than the rest. At the full stop, the pitch falls. He jots this down on his copy, and tries the singing again. This time he raises the pitch by a tone for the 'rust-' of 'rustles' and falls by a third and then a fourth for 'the' and 'trees'.

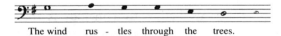

The wind   rus - tles   through   the   trees.

Example 4. 'The wind rustles through the trees', melody 1.

This is not the only set of pitches which would have done the job. He could just as well have used these pitches:

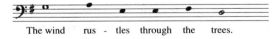

The wind   rus - tles   through   the   trees.

Example 5. 'The wind rustles through the trees', melody 2.

The audibility and meaning are better now, but still a few at the back of the church cannot hear. He cannot sing any louder without straining the voice again. So we move into third gear.

75

The Choir is Born

To double the volume we have two people singing at the same time. This makes performance of the song a little more complex. If the words are still to be clear, the singers must synchronize their rhythm. Unless they are the same, the two performers will be singing different words and both sets will be obscured. To help get things synchronized, they agree on pitch, and write the rhythm down.

Without knowing it, the basis of a whole system of musical notation and choral singing has been created. Everything else – part writing, instrumental support and so on – is icing on the cake.

From a simple idea, then, a method emerges. It is not there for its own sake, or to replace the idea, but to make it work. In practice, however, the method may be complex and need rehearsal. Such is musical performance that a systematic approach is required to achieve the proper working of even the simplest ideas in sound.

Beauty and the Beat

The addition of a clear rhythm to a melody is the first aid to singing together. Consider the plainsong melody 'Conditor alme siderum' which may be transcribed from the original notation as follows:

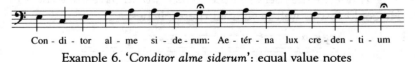

Con - di - tor   al - me   si - de - rum: Ae - tér - na   lux   cre - den - ti - um

Example 6. 'Conditor alme siderum': equal value notes

Compare that with the example below, which uses the same notes, but adds to them a clear and consistent rhythm.

The rhythmicized version will invariably be simpler for a group to sing together. Unfortunately, this may well result in a conflict

Con - di - tor al - me si - de-rum: Ae - tér - na lux cre - den - ti - um

Example 7. '*Conditor alme siderum*': rhythmic version

of interests between the meaning of the words (and the way they are accented), and the expediency of singing the words together. The natural stress of the first word, for example, is on its first syllable, *Con'-di-tor*. The rhythmicized version puts it on the second syllable, *Con-di'-tor*. So a degree of compromise and impurity is introduced whenever a piece of music, however simple, is sung simultaneously by two or more people.

The next stage in the development of song is the possibility of embellishment, either to make an aesthetically pleasing sound or to enhance or add to the meaning of the words. It was St Augustine who said that 'to sing is to pray twice', and he must have had in mind the repertoire of unaccompanied melodies which heighten the meaning of the words and add another dimension to them. This is another example, however, of the conflict between audibility and intelligibility. As a general rule, the more the meaning of the words is reflected in the shape and character of the music, through elaboration and decoration, the less audible the words themselves become.

Sense and Sensitivity

The dilemma may be understood differently in the context of a religious liturgy, which is designed specifically for repetition, and may therefore be pitched at a level slightly beyond that which may be grasped in a single hearing. If it is worth repeating at all, it is worth repeating for a reason, and that should be one of spiritual nourishment rather than one of mindless obedience to religious ritual.

The first point is that some parts of the liturgy are repeated over and over again, giving to specific texts a great familiarity over a period of time. In some traditions, it is usual to recite some parts of a service, such as the Lord's Prayer, in silence, even in communal worship. This is possible because of the familiarity of the text, and the likelihood that the time taken by individuals to say the particular words will be uniform, and that the sense of community will be heightened rather than lessened by the temporary absence of sound. The formulation of sound can have about it a feeling of automation which is given relief by a short period of structured silence, during which the mind and the liturgy continue, but the outward presentation of words ceases.

This extreme example makes the point that the audibility of the words may not be of overriding importance at every moment, especially if the worshipping community is constant and they share a more or less equal degree of familiarity.

The second point is to do with development and progress through repetition. When a good actor delivers his lines, he brings out different nuances and emphases at each performance, giving life and character to the words, through repetition. With music, the same can be achieved but with more possibilities. Not only can each piece of music be performed in a different way each time it is sung, but the same set of words can be sung to an infinite number of melodies and styles, each bringing different meaning.

Language is an incomplete and often imprecise means of communicating, especially in matters ethereal and divine. Music can be used to complement the words and provide a total meaning which is closer to the truth than they would be by themselves. This is, of course, dependent first upon the skill of the composer, and second upon the manner in which the music is performed.

So there is a choice to be made between the articulation and meaning of the words. It will be influenced by the make-up of the community or congregation, and by whether the music is intended as an evangelistic tool or as a form of sacrificial worship.

Mother Tongue

The judgement on audibility versus intelligibility is likely to have a bearing also on the acceptability of languages not spoken by members of the congregation. The traditional language for Christian worship in the West is Latin, which has served (and continues to serve in continental Europe) as a universal tongue, untouched either by the diversity of the vernacular, or by the rapid changes which are inclined to alter meaning and understanding. Latin holds its meaning for longer than the everyday languages: certain English words change their meaning completely over a period of time, and some constructions of even a hundred years ago seem outmoded and out of date. Where the Latin is used, however, an up-to-date translation ensures that the meaning of the words remains clear and contemporary, without altering any aspect of the original text. The Latin words can then be passed from generation to generation as part of a common religious language. A revival in the possibilities of Latin as a universal language has been brought about recently by its use within religious communities such as that at Taizé. Their chants are sung by pilgrims who travel from all parts of Europe and beyond, and for this reason the brothers have adopted Latin as their principal language.

To others, the use of a tongue no longer spoken anywhere in the world, as a means of public worship, seems bizarre and perverse. It seems to them that, of all possible languages, Latin should be last on the list. The preface to the 1662 Book of Common Prayer makes the point that:

> Whereas St Paul would have such language spoken to the people in the Church as they might understand, and have profit by hearing the same, the service in this Church of England these many years has been read in Latin to the people, which they understand not; so that they have heard with their ears only, and their heart, spirit, and mind, have not been edified thereby.

The use of Latin was very substantially reduced in the Catholic

Church after the second Vatican Council, and was prohibited by the Church of England (except in the universities where the language was understood) from the Reformation until recently.

The reasons for worshipping in the vernacular are not difficult to find, and it will always provide the most easily accessible medium for communication, provided it is accepted that wording may have to be altered from time to time in order to clarify meaning. As a rule, people are more likely to find a translation of a foreign text acceptable in worship than a paraphrase from antiquated to modern English, and not everyone is willing to pursue the meaning of defunct words for themselves.

In music, the question is whether the clarity of the words is the matter of primary concern, or whether the additional meaning which is made possible through it is sufficient to compensate either for a reduction in clarity or for the fact that the words belong to another age or tongue.

The Case for the Groaners

The human race is divided into two sexes, female and male. Some females have high voices and some have low voices. The same is true for males both before and after the age of puberty, although the natural range of boys and men is separated by an octave. The females with high voices have become known as sopranos and those with low voices as altos. The men with high voices are known as tenors and those with low voices as basses. The division with boys is the same as that with females, except that boy sopranos are usually called 'trebles'.

This is the basis for the four-part choir, and for the practice of part-writing in choral composition. The division of high and low within each sex is just as significant as the separation by an octave of the pitch ranges of women and men. It is quite usual, when singing a tune in unison with a large congregation, to find that a number of people will find the tune too low or too high.

Often there is no individual note which is too high, but after singing the melody several times (as is the case in a hymn tune), and therefore sustaining the range of pitch over a period of time, the voice becomes tired and begins to strain. The overall area of pitch which is responsible for this is known as the *tessitura*, and is somewhat different from the *range* of a melody. It would be possible to have two melodies of an identical range (that is to say the highest and lowest notes are identical) but one with a much higher tessitura than the other. If most of the melody is constructed towards the lower end of the range, then the tessitura is low, even though the range includes some high notes.

A soprano, treble or tenor, asked to sing a melody with a low tessitura would find themselves straining after a while, as they tried to force out notes which they find difficult to sing. The same would be true for an alto or bass who is asked to sing a melody with a high tessitura. For all singers, the most comfortable register for sustained singing is in the middle, when the extremities of range are not tested too often.

The practical effect of this anatomic fact is that it is difficult to write a melody to be sung in unison by all voices. In order to do so, the range of the majority of the melody needs to be so small that the melodic possibilities are very limited.

From the earliest times, therefore, people have divided themselves, often unconsciously, into high and low. Singing a high melody, those with lower voices will select a different starting pitch and sing all other notes relative to that. When applied to a single line, the result is known as *organum*. A melody of identical shape is sung simultaneously, in parallel, at two different pitches, divided by a perfect fourth or a perfect fifth. The sound of organum is one of the characteristic sounds of primitive medieval music.

What works with a single line, however, does not work with later hymns or songs which have been harmonized, and anyone who tries the organum effect while singing a hymn in church is likely to be rounded upon as a 'groaner'. Instead, these people will more usually drop down an octave for high notes and leap back up the octave for lower notes, thus compressing the range into a more manageable tessitura. Alternatively, they may simply leave out the sections of the melody which become too tiring to sing, or possibly give up altogether.

Who Sings the Tune?

The influence of the vocal tessitura on the suitability of sung music for a church depends upon the availability of a separate choir or group of singers, or, alternatively, the intention that the vocal music is for the whole congregation.

When it is meant for everyone, the melody must sit comfortably within the natural register of the whole congregation, otherwise it will cause discomfort to a proportion of people and bar them from participation. In this way, music becomes a frustrating and divisive, rather than uniting, force.

Where a group of singers is available within a church to form a choir, they will usually be divided into parts, soprano (or treble), alto, tenor and bass. As a shorthand, this is known as an SATB choir. In recent years, a number of parish churches have developed the use of a smaller singing group to lead songs and choruses which do not require part-singing. These tend to be small groups of a few singers only, whereas SATB choirs can include anything up to fifty or more members.

Voices Together

Having seen how music may be used to heighten the meaning of language, and having established the fact of the four basic tessituras of the human voice, the next thing is to reconcile the two and form them into a method of composition. The problem is that a melody which suits high voices will not also suit low voices, unless a starting pitch of a fourth or fifth lower is selected.

This may be solved in two ways, according to whether the voices are vertically or horizontally aligned. The first is that all parts start together, but the lower voices do not follow the shape of the melody. Instead, they form the harmonies above which the melody can be sung in the upper voice. This is known as 'homophony'. The homophonic style has the advantage that all voices, and therefore the words, are sounded together, giving some clarity of articulation. The disadvantage is that the lower voices are all denied the integrity of the possible marriage between music and words. The bass part (rather like a hymn tune) tends to hop up and down in fourths and fifths to define the harmonic basis of the melody, while the inner parts fill in the harmonies with as much flowing line as may be contrived.

By way of an example, the opening bars of the anthem 'If ye love me', by Thomas Tallis, may be used as a simple illustration. The soprano part follows the accents of the words precisely, with a rising phrase which gives emphasis to the two words 'love me', followed by a leap which coincides with the second syllable of the word 'commandments':

Example 8. 'If ye love me' (Tallis): soprano part

The bass part, on the other hand, in order to define the harmonic basis of the melody, does exactly the opposite:

Example 9. 'If ye love me' (Tallis): bass part

In this instance, the music of the bass part is serving the music of the soprano part rather than its own set of words, and therefore is one removed from the original intention of the music.

Imitation and Equality

The second solution is to retain the shape of the melody in all voices, but to start the parts at slightly different times. In this way, it is perfectly possible for the soprano's melodic line to be introduced to the alto part at a lower pitch, and so too with the remaining voices. This is known as a 'contrapuntal' or 'polyphonic' style (literally, 'many sounds'). Polyphony is choral music's answer to 'equal opportunities'. The advantage with this style is that each voice remains true to the words, and each voice plays an equal part in the texture of the music. The strictest form of such imitation is the round, or canon, in which the music of each part is identical throughout. This, however, is rare. The usual form of imitation is for the first few notes only to be the same or similar, before each phrase branches out into a melody which remains loosely imitative, but which accommodates the existence of the other parts around it.

As an example of the polyphonic style, let us look at two voices from the anthem 'Sing joyfully', by William Byrd. A comparison between the second soprano part and the first alto part shows that the music for the two voices is very similar, each following the thrust of the line demanded by the words, but the second part entering one bar later than the first.

Example 10. 'Sing joyfully' (Byrd): Soprano 2 and Alto 1

The disadvantage of the polyphonic style, however, is to do with clarity of words. One characteristic of all imitative music is that as each voice enters with a new line of music, so too is each layer of words overlaid with another. The point is very clearly heard in a simple canon such as '*Frère Jacques*'. As each voice enters the polyphony, the words naturally become less distinct, since two or more sets of words are being sung simultaneously. In a polyphonic work of some complexity, written in, say, six or more parts, it will be very difficult for a listener to identify many words after the first few bars.

Once again, the suitability of polyphonic music for any given church depends upon the judgement which is made on the balance between audibility and intelligibility. The homophonic style releases the words with a greater degree of clarity, whilst the polyphonic style allows the words a greater understanding through the music. It is all the more reason to know before you start to sing what the music is there to do. Is it to evangelize, to unite, or to worship God?

CHAPTER 6

Musical Instruments

'They should have stuck to strings as we did, and kept out clarinets and done away with serpents. If you'd thrive in musical religion, stick to strings, says I.'
'Strings be safe soul-lifters, as far as that do go,' said Mr Spinks.
(Thomas Hardy, *Under the Greenwood Tree*)

Hardy's father and grandfather were players in the church bands at Stinsford and Puddletown in Dorset. His father belonged to the same generation as Anthony Trollope and Samuel Sebastian Wesley. By his time, church bands were robustly independent and proud of their status within the community. So while the cathedral choirs which Wesley lamented were in disarray, the bands of the rural churches were at their height. So the cycle turns.

Because of the tradition built up since then, it is easy now to assume that the organ has always been the dominant musical instrument in churches. This is not even the case in Britain, and it certainly is not in other parts of Europe.

In Germany, from the medieval period through to the end of the eighteenth century, skilled orchestral musicians were part of the regular weekly worship in most major town churches, an arrangement which came about through the widespread co-operation of civic and church authorities. Bach, for example, as part of his official duties as cantor of St Thomas's Church in Leipzig, was called upon to write an instrumental cantata for every Sunday and feast day of the liturgical year. Similar duties were required of dozens of other town and church musicians. A core of instrumentalists were placed on the civic payroll, supplemented by others where necessary, and were available to the cantor for church use every Sunday. For the most part, the organ, though important in baroque Germany, played little part in the accompaniment of voices. It had a much greater use as a solo instrument which could be used to reflect and inspire the mood of a service through the use of the art of improvisation.

In England the regular use of highly trained and skilled instrumentalists in church worship has never been so organized or as commonplace as it was in Germany, and was more or less limited to the music of the Chapel Royal in the seventeenth and eighteenth centuries. The verse anthems of Henry Purcell, for example, were written for the set-up there.

Much more widespread in England was the use of the 'folk' instrumentalists as described by Hardy, in the form of 'West Gallery Bands' which flourished from the end of the seventeenth century until the middle of the nineteenth century, and which, after about a hundred and fifty years' absence, appear to be making something of a comeback.

Such groups today may be termed 'worship bands' or 'praise bands', and their function is usually to lead the music of the huge corpus of folk- and popular-style songs which has grown up over the last two decades. In addition, and because they are established in the church, they sometimes accompany other parts of the music such as hymns.

Which Instruments Shall We Have?

Traditionally, instruments are divided into three main categories: strings, wind and percussion. Further divisions can then be made according to how they are played. In addition to the natural sounds, electronic instruments add to the selection available today. Before deciding which instruments, if any, should be used in church, first decide what they are needed for. Because they cannot be used to articulate ideas with the same clarity as the human voice, instruments in churches usually come in conjunction with some form of vocal music. They may *lead* singing, *accompany* it, or may be used independently. Independent use usually occurs only before and after a service and at various restricted times within it, but the leading and accompanying roles are common throughout a service.

If the role of the instruments is to lead singing, do they do so by themselves, or in conjunction with a choir? If it is the latter, they are, in a way, a halfway house between leading and accompanying. They are accompanying the choir but as part of a greater body of musicians who together are leading the remainder of the congregation.

Two flutes and a harp may make a beautiful combination to accompany a gentle solo song, but they will not be sufficient to lead a large choir and congregation in a stirring hymn. Conversely, a strong bass guitar and drum kit may help greatly in leading a large congregation in a modern song, but would be out of place in a reflective hymn.

All Together Now

The musical derivation of folk bands is deliberately secular, and often introduced with an eye to gentle evangelism. At St Mary's Barchester, the worship band was introduced in order to attract people to church, or at least not to alienate them from it. The church decided that the musical style should match the culture of the day, to offer a reassuring and familiar element to Christianity which can be shared immediately without training or initiation. In this way, the concentration of teaching may be focused on the word of God, without the distraction of either the acquisition of musical expertise or learning to appreciate it. The style of much of the music heard at St Mary's is deliberately ephemeral, and designed to be discarded after a period of time.

The make-up of the band there is defined by the players who

happen to be available in the congregation, rather than as a result of any master plan. Consequently, it is a very unconventional group, musically speaking, and would normally be thought to lack coherence or balance.

The speed with which worship bands have built up and become commonplace has caught church musicians unawares, and only now are some of the basic needs of such groups being addressed.

What's the Score?

The first requirement is that the player needs to know what notes to play and when. The first duty of any director of music preparing for an instrumental performance, therefore, is either to assemble a set of parts, or else to divide up a full score and write them out.

In this respect, instruments can be divided into two types: melody and harmony instruments. Melody instruments are those essentially capable of playing only one line at a time. This category includes the flute, oboe, clarinet, trumpet, horn, violin and cello. Harmony instruments are those capable of sounding more than one pitch, either simultaneously or in such rapid succession as to make up a chord. These include all keyboard instruments, such as the piano, synthesizer and organ, and guitar and harp. Harmony instruments can play the melody too, although they are usually less successful when used exclusively in this way. Additionally, percussion instruments are used to bolster the rhythm.

. The West Gallery Bands appear to have operated under a fairly strict system of four-part harmony, in which each part was played by one or more melody instruments and sung simultaneously by a group of singers. They would gather round the instrument playing their part, which would support the vocalists, many of whom did not read music, and give them a firm lead. The instruments, then, were used as a means of vocal doubling, and not as an independent musical force. No harmony instruments were used at all.

To this extent, the modern counterpart of the West Gallery Band differs considerably. The most common form of musical presentation of folk- and pop-type music since the 1970s has been in what may be termed a 'short score'. This means that the melody line is written out in full, together with a simple, bare-bones piano accompaniment in a variable number of parts, and a chord sequence which roughly corresponds to the piano part. The advantage with this form of presentation is that it appears simple, unfussy and infinitely adaptable. The disadvantage is that the music does not usually indicate exactly which notes are to be played. In order to be performed at all, it *has* to be adapted or arranged.

As with the new proposals at St Mary's, this demands the skill of an arranger who has a good grasp of the music, a good working knowledge of the instruments at her disposal, and the considerable amount of time needed to write out parts for each of the players. As a minimum requirement, then, the music may be performed with keyboard accompaniment alone. Its style, however, usually demands some more imaginative treatment to allow it to be heard to best effect, and this is where some degree of 'orchestration' is called for. If there is a choir, there is some extra writing to be done for them, since, for reasons explained in the previous chapter, it is not ideal for a four-part choir to be singing in unison for long periods.

The style of music and the range of possibilities will depend upon the combination and types of instrument available, and this in turn will determine the extent to which a musical arrangement, or orchestration, is required. At St Swithun's Upper Barchester, the group consists entirely of harmony instruments: they have a piano, three guitars and sometimes a percussionist. For them, very little arrangement is called for. The guitars play from the chord sequence printed in the copies, and the pianist (the only trained musician among them) uses the same sequence as the basis of a simple improvised part. The piano provides as much melody part as is required, the guitars sustain the chords and add some rhythm; the percussionist gives a bit more rhythm to it when he is there. The function of the harmony instruments is much the same as that of the accordion in an outside dance band, in that it provides a simple statement of the basic harmonic progression, and indeed the musical effect is not dissimilar.

To have a look at what they do, let us take a simple melody:

Example 11. 'Glory and all honour': melody with short score

The pianist plays from the part, vamping as he goes along:

Example 12. 'Glory and all honour': improvised piano part

Meanwhile, the guitarists add the chords, and supply a degree of rhythmic interest, perhaps using the rhythm:

Example 13. 'Glory and all honour': guitar rhythm

Simple though such an arrangement is, someone still has to decide how the music shall start and finish, especially if it is being used to lead a congregation. People brought up on hymns are used to a 'playover', that is, the first or last part of the hymn on the organ alone, followed by a short and predictable gap, after which the music is repeated, this time with choir and congregation. The organist decides which part of the hymn should be chosen as the playover, and can judge how long the pause should be. This decision involves just one person. With a group, however, it is important to agree a method of establishing a communal speed, starting together, finishing together, and restarting together after a playover or the end of a verse. An alternative, and usually more effective, method is for a short introduction or linking passage to be written which does away with the need for a pause. This, however, needs to be composed, written out in advance and parts distributed to all the players.

Combining Instruments

The administration of instrumental musicians is extremely complex, because of the difficulty in sorting out the mechanics of music-making. There are a few combinations of instruments which have attracted such a large repertoire of music that a permanent ensemble can be brought together to perform it. A string quartet is one of them. They will find music written for them by most of the great composers from the classical period to the present day. It is easy to imagine that the make-up of a symphony orchestra is similarly standard, but this is far from being the case. Orchestral managers constantly have to deal with the fact that different orchestral works are scored for very different combinations of instruments.

Most orchestral works include a nucleus of strings – first and second violins, viola, cello and double bass – but the woodwind and brass sections vary a good deal, according to whether clarinets, horns, trumpets, trombones and so on are included or not, and if so, how many. The possibilities for percussion combinations are even wider and more difficult to manage. The manager of the CBCO has to decide whether it will be better to employ a certain instrumental player as a full-time member of staff, but then not to use her for some pieces, or whether to 'buy in' a player each time that instrument is required.

The variety stems from the fact that different works require different sounds or timbres, specified according to the composer's intention. On the whole, his instrumentation is not interchangeable with another. It would not be possible for an oboist to play from a clarinet part, for example, for three reasons: first, the clarinet is capable of sounding several bass notes which are not available on an oboe; second, a passage which may lie easily under the fingers of a clarinettist may be awkward for an oboist; and third, the clarinet is one of a group of instruments known as 'transposing' instruments. This means that the instrument sounds a note which is different from the written pitch. A B-flat clarinet, for example, will sound one tone lower than the written pitch. An oboist playing a clarinet part, therefore, would end up playing the part a tone high, and would be at odds with all the other players.

The Mechanics

The quantity of paperwork and organization in dealing with instrumental music is cumbersome. Imagine, for example, the performance of one simple chord of C major, first played on the organ, and second by the small group of instrumentalists they have at St Mary's, namely violin, cello, horn, oboe and clarinet.

The organist is shown a chord which looks like this:

Example 14. Chord of C major: organ part

She duly places her fingers over the correct keys, depresses them, and plays the chord.

93

The same piece of paper, however, is not sufficient to achieve a performance of the same chord by the instrumental group. Before it can be played, three things must happen. First, someone with sufficient experience needs to decide how the five notes shall be distributed among the instruments. The chord will sound very different if the horn-player takes the top note, for example, from the sound which will be made if the violin takes the top note and the horn a lower one. The person making that decision also has to know which instruments are capable of producing the notes in question.

The second thing is that the notes are divided up into separate parts. There are three reasons for this: one is that the instruments may require different dynamic markings, since some are naturally quieter than others, for the sounds to blend into one coherent chord. Second, the clarinettist and the horn-player will require their parts to be written in a different key, so that the note they produce sounds at the correct pitch. Third, the five notes need to be written on five pieces of paper, since the playing space of each instrumentalist demands that they cannot stand together and use a single copy. The set of parts may look like this:

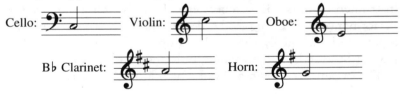

Example 15. Chord of C major: instrumental parts. Note that of these five common instruments, only the oboe and violin share both clef and key signature.

Finally, some way must then be found to ensure that the instrumentalists play together. This may involve a sixth person giving a downbeat which all the players can see. The performance of a well-played orchestral work shows how the result is well worth the effort, but it is easy to see that the involvement of instrumentalists is not to be taken on lightly.

An alternative to this apparently laborious method is not easy to find. Had the five players been shown the C major chord and asked to play, it could probably be assumed that the cellist would automatically have selected the lowest note, but no such assumption could be made of the other players. Even if the horn-player and clarinettist were happy to make a transposition themselves, it is extremely unlikely that the four instruments would have selected one each of the remaining four notes.

It is important to appreciate the degree of complexity, not to avoid using instruments, but to ensure that, if they are to be used, they are used to good effect. One of the problems at St Mary's is that, up until now, no parts have ever been provided for their instrumentalists to use. The same short score has been given to all the players, who were asked to 'busk' their parts as best they might. Most of the melody instruments took the tune, because it is the only complete line and much the easiest to read. The transposing instruments had the worst time of all. Without parts, they had to make the transposition as they went along, which they found extremely difficult. They had to concentrate so hard to get any notes at all which were correct, that there was no time to do anything interesting. They often made mistakes, and no one realized how difficult this 'simple' tune was for them. Sadly, the effect was chaotic and wholly unrewarding.

Writing for Instruments

The example of the C major chord demonstrates the degree of thought and preparation necessary in order to achieve even a minimal result. Preparing a whole piece of music for performance with instrumental accompaniment is clearly a much greater task, but, because few written parts are available commercially, and since in any case the repertoire changes quickly, it is a skill which is often called for.

Let us see how a melody might be developed. It starts life as a tune written out in short score.

Example 16. 'Master, speak!': melody and short score

Given to a pianist, he would make something of it, in the way we showed before. But give it to the five instrumentalists at St Mary's and it is no use at all. They have no idea what to play. The cellist, I suppose, is safe enough, because he can play the lowest line. The only other part which is complete is the melody. The other inner parts are merely filling in the chords, sometimes with three extra notes, sometimes with one, but there are no other lines which are complete. It is not possible, therefore, to say to the oboist 'you take the second line down' or to the clarinettist 'you take the third line down', because there are too many parts missing in the score. Furthermore, the clarinet and horn need the music to be written in different keys. So, the director of music composes and writes out a set of instrumental parts:

Example 17. 'Master, speak!': basic score of instrumental parts

At least the music can now be played. Essentially, the oboe, horn and violin are being used to make up the basic chords with the melody in the oboe part, while the clarinet – the only instrument with any interest – adds a sense of movement with some quaver arpeggio passages.

Using the same parts for several verses becomes dull, and the congregation begins to cry out for some variety. So for the next verse – which is played more quietly – the ensemble is rescored. This time the clarinet has the melody, while the oboe plays a counter-melody, or 'descant'. The other instruments make up the harmony.

Example 18. 'Master, speak!': descant arrangement for instruments

Usually the instruments are used in conjunction with a keyboard instrument and some singers. Then they are released from the need to 'lead' the singing, and can be used to embellish the sound and add interest to the music. At St Mary's, the organ will soon be available in addition to the five instruments. The singing group has the melody while the organist plays a specially-written accompaniment:

Example 19. 'Master, speak!': organ part

Musically, the singers and organ together are sufficient. The arranger is free, therefore, to write a set of instrumental parts which are more idiomatic for the particular instruments.

Example 20. 'Master, speak!': freely-written instrumental parts

Musical Chairs

Having achieved a set of parts for the five players, it is time to turn to the preparation of a performance. The first thing to think about is how the players stand or sit. The cellist is the only player who has to sit down in order to play the instrument. All the others can play standing or sitting. This is something which may be decided by the space available, since a great deal of room is saved if instrumental players stand. On the other hand, if the instrumental group is used at several different points during a service, it may be distracting if they have to keep moving about. If they are given seats, they may remain in set positions throughout the service, and may therefore be more discreet.

Each player (or pair of them if there are two using the same copy) will require a music stand. Again, this takes up space, and should be measured out or set out well in advance of a rehearsal to be sure that the instrumentalists are not cramped. The cellist, additionally, needs either a rough floor surface, or a wooden T, or perhaps a bit of old carpet, so that the cello spike can be rested on the floor without it either slipping or doing damage to the surface.

Parts written, stands set out, and the rehearsal is almost ready to begin. The remaining task is to check that the instruments are in tune with each other. When there is no keyboard instrument involved, the oboe will sound an A, and the others tune to that. When there is a keyboard instrument, the others always tune to it. It is worth checking the pitch of the keyboard instrument at a very early stage of planning. There are, in particular, many organs which are not tuned to anything like standard concert pitch, and this can cause huge problems for instrumentalists. For an oboe, for example, there is a physical limit to the degree of pitch variation which is available, and if the organ is tuned very high, the oboist will never be able to reach the pitch, and the two instruments can never be used together. This fact sometimes comes as a surprise, and disappointment, to would-be ensembles who have for years been unaware that the church organ is tuned high or low.

Administration

Because the preparation of parts is so laborious and time-consuming, they should be kept carefully and filed for reuse. In this way, the musical director's workload, over a period of time, will be reduced. One of the frustrations, however, is the difficulty of keeping a constant group together. Suppose, for example, that in our ensemble of five players, the horn-player and the oboist are a husband and wife who move away from the area. Suddenly, the group is diminished to only three players, a violin, clarinet and cello. Soon afterwards, two other people come forward, one a trumpeter, and the other, another clarinettist. The trumpet is another transposing instrument, but works at a different transposition from the horn (see Appendix A), so cannot be given the horn part to play. The range and timbre of the instrument is also quite different and an idiomatic horn part cannot be transferred to the trumpet.

The presence of a second clarinettist presents a different problem, in that it is not especially desirable to have two clarinettists doubling the same part when all the other parts are played by a single instrument. The oboe part could be adapted for a second clarinet, but new copies would have to be prepared in the correct transposition key, and some of the original intentions of the scoring would be compromised by the new arrangement.

Imagine then that a similar switch of instruments happened twice again in the course of three or four years, and it is easy to see how a musical director can, after some years of work, be left with a set of parts which is now inappropriate for all the instruments at her disposal, and therefore finds herself effectively back to square one. The frustration is further compounded by the deliberately ephemeral nature of much of the music, which means that an arrangement may be used on a limited number of occasions before the piece loses its popularity and falls out of use. The fragment of a piece used in the example above lasts about eight seconds, and has already involved quite a lot of work. For a piece lasting two or three minutes, a lot of work is lost when it falls out of use. The reverse of this situation has its own dangers, that a piece could continue to be used after its freshness has worn off, only because instrumental parts are available for it. In this case, the system has the effect of prolonging a piece beyond its natural life span.

Program for Problems

One of the bright spots in this situation is the development of computer programs which can print out extra parts and transpose them at the touch of a button. This has limited application, of course, since the parts have to be written in the first place, and it can lead to the temptation to ignore the idiomatic style of an instrument if, say, a trumpet part is transposed and given to a violin. Nevertheless, used sensibly it can do much to relieve the burden of a musical director who is faced with a changing or inconsistent ensemble and the resultant problems of rescoring items on a weekly basis.

A further development is found in the possibilities presented by the Musical Instrument Digital Interface (MIDI) system, in which a part may be played on an electronic keyboard, and effectively transcribed into print through the program. Again, this is a time-saving device which can greatly assist in the preparation of parts, although it hardly need be said that such systems are very expensive.

Making Progress

There are a number of factors which make the long-term development of an instrumental ensemble within a church a very considerable challenge. The first is the likelihood that musicians will change over a period of time, and that they will be replaced by people who play different instruments.

The second factor is that the technical progress of players is likely to depend upon tuition received outside church commitments, and there may well be a mixture of young musicians in the process of learning, and who therefore improve over a period of years, alongside those who have learned to play an instrument years before but who have now given it up bar their playing in church. These people are unlikely to improve significantly, therefore, over any period of time. It is not realistic to expect players to learn a great deal technically from other instrumentalists, and in this respect they differ from singers. It is quite possible for a bass singer to learn from a soprano, but it is very unlikely that any technical knowledge of horn-playing will be learnt from a violinist.

The third factor, related to the second, is that a musical director is limited by the possibilities of training. Whereas with a choir it is possible to execute training exercises in which all can participate, the same is not true of instruments, each of which has different requirements and therefore their own routines.

The fourth factor is one of balance, and the choice which will often have to be made between excluding people who wish to be included, and having a well-balanced group. There is not usually room for more than one drummer, for example, in a band. The same may apply to ability. It is quite out of the question to include a player with no previous training on an instrument. In general, the range of abilities offered is likely to be wide, from, say, a local music teacher with great experience to a beginner with very little. Players of vastly differing capabilities do not always combine well.

The King of Instruments

The organ has reigned supreme in churches in England now for a little over a hundred years. It has the capacity to offer a huge range of sounds, in both timbre and volume, in crude imitation of the orchestral possibilities, yet played by a single player. This is a strength as well as a weakness. For a good musical result combined with administrative simplicity, the organ is an excellent option, and doubtless that is why it has achieved continued popularity.

The organ is a collection of complete ranks of pipes, each pipe corresponding to one note on the keyboard or pedal board. The pipes may be made of wood or metal, they may be stopped or open, and they may be blown more like flutes or more like a reed instrument. All these factors have a bearing on the sound. Each rank of pipes may be brought into play or left silent at any one time, and each is operated by a 'stop' which is controlled at the organ console. An instrument of even moderate size should contain some long, and therefore low, pipes, which are good for supporting congregational singing. It will also contain some very small pipes, high in pitch, which can be used to give rhythmic impetus. There will probably be some stops which can be used as solo sounds, and others which are good for quiet accompaniment.

By now, a considerable repertoire of choral and organ music has been written, and there is therefore plenty of music immediately ready to be sung and played. If time is limited, as it usually is, this can be used to fulfil more musical matters and fewer matters of administration and paperwork.

The organ, however, has its limitations. It is not a naturally rhythmic instrument, partly because the sound is sustained rather than decaying as the sound of a piano will do, and it is hardly ever the appropriate instrument for folk music, or any style which calls for 'vamping' or free playing of chord progressions. Pianistic writing does not transfer well to the organ, and if a piano part is to be played on the organ, it is usually necessary to recompose the music completely and write it out fully.

The organ is also a necessarily exclusive instrument, because it is played by just one person. In churches where there are instrumentalists of high calibre, they are naturally left out of the musical life of the church. Equally, if the organist is a poor player, it follows that all the music will suffer. In an instrumental group, on the other hand, one poor player may be masked by the skill of others.

For all that, the organ will probably continue to have a central role in church worship for many years. It will always be easier to find an organist than an instrumental band, for example, for a funeral or any other service arranged at short notice.

Electronic Instruments

In recent years, growing use has been made in churches of electronic instruments and amplified acoustic instruments and voices. These demand the same considerations as any other instruments in the way air is moved around the church in the form of sound waves.

In the process of producing an electronic sound, there are two points of particular importance: the *sound source* and the *sound production*. The sound source may be acoustic or electronic, but the sound production will always be a loudspeaker, or a pair of loudspeakers. In between the two, there will be an amplifier. If the sound source is acoustic, there will also be a microphone.

The success of electronic instruments in a church (including an electronic organ) depends most of all upon the type, number and positioning of loudspeakers. It is common among church rock bands to find speakers being used in a large building which were designed for small-scale domestic use. The temptation then is to over-amplify the sound to make up for the deficiencies in the loudspeakers. The size of a pair of loudspeakers capable of moving the quantity of air which is moved by the largest organ pipe will be very large, and may be unsightly, but it may nonetheless be necessary to cater for the size of the church.

Investing in the Future

The instruments which are used in a church may define the whole character of the worship within it, and therefore careful thought is essential.

The first stage is to think about the acoustic properties of the church. It is very unlikely that the same building will be suitable for choral singing of polyphonic music (with no instruments at all) and also for a rock band. The reverberance which enhances one will destroy the other. This single consideration may remove the need for further discussion, but if several options are still open, the following must be taken into account: the purpose of the instruments; the space available for them; the number of players available; and the system within which they will be used.

Of all of these, the system is perhaps the most important. I have tried to outline the complexities involved for even the simplest use of instrumental ensembles. The choice of instruments is not the sort of decision that can be made as though it were the choice of groceries in a supermarket. It is much more like choosing a mortgage: it is a decision which must be binding for a period, and if the commitment is broken, a considerable loss of investment will result.

CHAPTER 7

Finishing Touches

The violinist at St Mary's Barchester is tuning up, and things are looking promising today. She is standing in her position, she has a music stand with a specially-written violin part and is all set to play. The structure so far has worked well. But before she comes to perform the music, there are one or two other things which still need to be looked after. She has to go through it to work out how the notes shall be performed: whether she will be playing 'up bow' or 'down bow', and which notes she will run together. The dynamic markings, loud and soft, may already be in the part, but if they are not, she will have to mark those in too. Many notes on the violin can be played in several ways, with different fingerings on different strings, so she needs to work these out, especially if there are any difficult passages.

After the structure and the mechanics are in place, the music is ready to be played, and musicianship and technique take over. These are acquired by tuition and experience and are vital ingredients for any musical performance. Broadly speaking, technique goes with accuracy and musicianship goes with spirit.

Calling the Tune

The single factor which is common to almost every type of group rehearsal is that there needs to be at least one person who knows exactly what is required, and who has an end result in her mind's ear. It is that person's job to impart that knowledge in as fast and clear a way as possible, through the copies of music which each individual has, through additional verbal instructions, and finally through physical gesture in rehearsal or performance. Before expanding on those three methods, I should say first that the lack of any such person will always make for a slow, hesitant and unfulfilling rehearsal. It is not a question of dictatorship against democracy, but simply one of leadership. Democracy can underpin everything she does: she listens to others' views as she prepares, and afterwards she listens to other opinions. But when it comes to rehearsal, clear direction is called for, not random ideas and 'committee' judgements.

Are We Ready?

The first stage is to decide what is to be performed. We have already established that the structure will dictate what genres and styles of music are possible. Within those parameters, specific choices now have to be made, based first on which voices and instruments are available. A second factor is one of difficulty, and this is something which is most easily judged with experience and with the benefit of musicianship. It is sometimes the case that music which is technically very simple is the most difficult to perform musically. Amateur choirs of average ability, such as that at St Peter's, are often at their best when singing music which is bold and rhythmic, rather than that which is gentle and ethereal, even though the rhythmic music may require a little more learning initially.

The next stage is for the musical director to know the music. Music should never be learned, as it were, 'on the choir' or orchestra, and it is not up to a choir to teach him the music. It is surprising how often this happens, however, even among professional musicians. Once he knows the music, the musical director is in a position to go through the score looking for practical details. This may include such details as breathing points, dynamic markings, time changes, methods of starting and finishing together, and so on. If there are two pieces to be sung in succession, the musical director may also think about pitch and consider whether the keys will match, or whether one piece should be transposed.

All of these practical decisions should be marked into his score. Often there is more than one acceptable solution to a performance problem which arises: if a breath has to be taken between phrases, for example, he may either reduce the value of the duration of one chord in order to allow time for the breath, or else put extra time into the music between the phrases. Either solution is acceptable, but a group of musicians needs to know which decision has been taken in order that they may all do the same thing. If they do not know, there is likely to be a moment of chaos at that point, while different musicians make contradictory assumptions.

Taking Note

The next stage is to transfer the instructions marked in the director's score into the minds of all performers. In practice, transferring the information to their minds means first transferring the information to their copies. There are two opposite ways of doing this. The quickest way to give a clear direction is to mark it in the copies. If it has to be written into each copy by the musical director, however, it is the slowest method for him. He can bypass the preparatory work by choosing to make the necessary announcements, but only by taking time in the rehearsal. Let us see what happens at St Peter's.

They have a choir of twenty-four singers. Mr Singer, the choirmaster, wants to change a dynamic marking from loud to soft, a direction which he has already indicated in his own score, but which is not in the printed copies. So he takes them away before the rehearsal and replaces 'f' (*forte*) with 'p' (*piano*) in each of them. In the rehearsal, however, he decides on another change. So he makes an announcement during rehearsal, and waits while each person marks it in his copy.

The contrast between the two methods is unexpectedly severe. No one even thought about how the first marking had got into the copies. They just sang quietly instead of loudly as their copies asked them to do. Everyone has the same indication, and at the correct place. No one has any idea how long it took Mr Singer to change all the copies.

The second marking does not go unnoticed. There is some confusion in the alto line as to which *forte* mark is to be changed. One of the altos has altered the wrong one, and is now trying to borrow a rubber, which she has not got. No one seems to have one. Half the trebles have lost their pencils, and young Peter, who has found his, is annoyed to find that its lead has been broken. One of the men puts up his hand to point out that two of the basses are away today, and offers to mark up their copies too. Kitty in the front row thinks she should change Gill's copy, and they go over to the cupboards to find the missing people's copies. Initially, it was much quicker for Mr Singer, but in the end, the total human time taken has been much greater.

Either method may be made more efficient through the introduction of system. The first may be made easier if the task of marking up copies can be shared among two or three individuals who are reliable, and who have time to devote to this.

The second may be made to work better if the choir is disciplined, is expecting such instructions and is prepared for them, and if the musical director is consistent about the way instructions are given. If a singer is ready with a pencil, and receives the instruction, 'Page 4, top line, third bar, soprano part, please change the marked dynamic from *forte* to *piano*,' then the change will not take long to effect. If, on the other hand, an instruction is given about singing the 'Alleluia' a bit softer than marked, and invites the response, 'Which Alleluia is that?', followed by long-distance pointing to copies, comparing notes and discussing the merits of the change, then the whole operation takes a considerable time.

All this is another part of the mechanics of music. By oiling the mechanics, the machine works more smoothly. By dealing with the mechanics of music-making efficiently, the benefits may be heard in sound. In practical terms, this is about the degree of expectation demanded from the choir. Are they expected to have pencils ready? Are they expected to be listening?

To some, such attention to the mechanics of music may seem fussy, petty and military rather than musical, but the reverse is in fact the case. A simple instruction such as that in my example can take anything up to one minute to complete, by the time the flow of rehearsal has been stopped, the instruction has been made, the copies have been marked, and the flow has been resumed. If fifteen such changes are made in the course of a rehearsal, then a quarter of an hour has been taken up which could have been spent on music. This is what is to be avoided.

With instrumentalists there is an additional reason to mark up copies for them, which is that it is difficult for them to have a pencil at the ready in the way a singer can because they usually have to put their instruments down first and sometimes remove the copy from the music stand.

The direction of the whole process, then, begins in the mind of the director. It is transferred from his mind to his copy, to the copies of other musicians, and finally to the minds of the whole group. Laborious though this may be, there is no very satisfactory short cut. Some people try to work on the system of hopeful telepathy, going straight from mind to mind with no stages in between, but unfortunately this does not work.

Training or Co-ordinating

There is wide scope for variation in the relationship between the musical director and the musicians of the church. In some churches the director will have a training role, in others he will have a mainly co-ordinating role, while in others there will be a mixture of both elements. The extent to which training is possible depends partly upon the ability of the director and partly upon the ability and the potential of the church's musicians.

Choirs lend themselves to training much more than instrumental groups. Even the very finest cathedral choirs recruit members who have very little expertise. The boys at Barchester Cathedral usually audition at the age of about seven or eight. By this time, only a small amount of ability will have shown itself either in terms of vocal technique or in sight-singing, but Mr Morgan is looking for potential and a readiness to learn.

This, however, is set in the context of an intensive training over a period of years, and it is some time before a new chorister is allowed to sing a service. At the cathedral, of course, Mr Morgan is an excellent musician and is able to instruct the new choristers. They also learn by example.

The same may also be true of older members in parish choirs, where previous singing experience is not automatically a requirement for membership. An inexperienced but committed and dedicated choir member who is willing to attend rehearsals and learn, is usually more valuable than an experienced singer whose appearance is sporadic and who is unreliable.

These are qualities which lend themselves to a religious attitude and way of life and it is a happy coincidence that the same qualities which are needed for religious observance are also those which are most valuable for members of a musical system.

Rehearsing Choirs

It is not enough to say that singers have the facility to convey words: singers cannot do without them. These days, choirs need words more than words need choirs. The functional ways in which choirs may once have served the words, as a means of amplification, are now superseded. Generally speaking, choral singing is not the best way to communicate words. If words are to be heard in a large building today, a good public address system will enhance the spoken voice with a much greater clarity than any endeavour in choral music will ever achieve.

Nevertheless, there is another purpose in singing beyond the functional duties to do with amplification. Sterile words express only part of a meaning. Even in ordinary speech, the meaning of a single word can be radically altered by changes in pitch, volume and length. If the word 'really' is delivered at a loud volume and at a high, ascending pitch, it becomes an excited exclamation – 'really?!' – the sort of word you might use when you are told your friend has just won the pools. The same word, delivered gently, at a low pitch, but still ascending has a suspicious ring about it – 'really?' – the sort of word you might use when your small son, caught next to the wall, pen in hand, tells you he was not just about to scribble on it. 'Really!' can be a word of disapproval, when it is delivered at high volume but descending pitch. The same word has diverse meanings according to its music. When people talk about music enhancing the words, therefore, it is more than a prettification of them, it is about adding another layer of meaning.

Words are made up of a combination of consonants and vowel sounds. Vowels may be sung, whereas consonants may not. Because singing is louder than speaking, the vowel sounds are usually louder than consonants, particularly than the so-called 'soft' consonants such as 'v' and 'f' (as opposed to the 'hard' 't' and 'k'). Furthermore, the length of a vowel may be indefinitely extended, while that of a consonant cannot. A 't' sound, for example, cannot be extended: its very character comes from its short, sharp duration. There are some middle ground consonants, such as 'm' and 'l' which can be extended up to a point, but not as successfully as the vowel sounds.

These vowel sounds present their own difficulties. In the English language, some are pure, such as 'e' (as in 'egg'), and some are combinations, or 'diphthongs', such as 'a' (as in 'ate') which is 'e' plus 'i'. Vowels are produced with an open mouth, and are dictated by the shape of the mouth. Sometimes the difference is very small, and laziness causes them to become indistinct or indistinguishable.

The danger, therefore, is for words to become distorted through singing, as part of a word becomes too loud and overwhelms another part. At worst, singing can become a series of indistinguishable vowel sounds which obliterate the consonants. In this way the words are neither properly formed nor heard, and their meaning is lost, not only to those who listen, but also to those who sing.

The introduction of a method is useful in avoiding these dangers. Vowels need to be pure, and consonants need to be neat. If there is a diphthong to sing, it is useful to work out at which point the vowel changes from one to another. If there is a consonant to place, the choir needs to know whether it should come on the beat, on the half-beat or just before the beat. The more that can be marked into copies, the better.

Preparing for an Instrumental Rehearsal

With instrumental groups, the ratio of rehearsal and preparation time spent on mechanics to that spent on music is inclined to be weighted further towards the mechanics, and this is a tendency which needs to be streamlined. Setting up musical instruments always takes longer than setting up singers: there are music stands to put up, 'playing room' to find and instruments to tune. With the increase in the use of electronics in instrumental music, more time still is taken in making sure that circuits are sound, 'howlround' is avoided and so on. It is useful for each player to know how long he realistically takes to set up an instrument, so that each member can arrive in time to be ready for a set starting time. This means that individuals are asked to put in the extra time required to enable the whole group to take full advantage of their time together. Otherwise it is easy to let ten minutes of valuable time slip away while one member lays out, plugs in or sets up his musical instrument.

'Informal' Music

Music of the dance band type played in the context of an 'informal' or non-liturgical service often seems to lend itself to more informal rehearsal, largely because there tend to be fewer people involved – perhaps four or five, rather than a choir of twenty people. On this subject, I would merely raise the caveat that an informal result is not necessarily achieved by informal preparation. Just as good comedians work hard, and often seriously, to make sure that the result will make other people laugh, so too with musicians who wish to make other people feel at ease. People do not feel at ease if the musicians who are leading them appear to be at odds, and the onus remains on the musicians to rehearse and perform to the best of their ability.

Bringing Groups Together

When different groups of musicians work separately within a church, it requires a different skill again to bring the groups together into a single performance. The skill is acquired by a knowledge of how the individual groups work, what they have in common and what they do differently.

Once a year, St Peter's and St Swithun's have a combined service which is held at St Peter's. For this service they bring together the choir at St Peter's with the folk group at St Swithun's. Bringing the two forces together calls for some creative compromise.

The folk group players usually 'busk' their parts, which is perfectly possible with harmony instruments. The first year they came together, they were very surprised that the choir were not able to do the same. 'There's nothing fancy,' said the leader. 'We just play and you just sing.' It turned out that the tune went up to a top F sharp, well beyond the range of the basses and some of the altos, and there were no other parts for the choir. In the end, the sopranos sung the piece on their own, but the leader was left bewildered. 'Why couldn't they just sing it?' he wondered. 'Were

114

they being difficult?' The choir, because of its size, is used to following the pace and instructions of the choirmaster, whereas the players (with only four in number) usually like to discuss points amongst themselves. A time which was meant to create unity and harmony ended up with division and irritation. For future services, music has been chosen carefully, parts prepared and each group rehearses separately before the two come together. Unity and fellowship are now the hallmarks. The people are the same. The only thing that has changed is in the planning: due consideration is given to the practicalities and mechanics of making music.

Rehearsal is probably the most creative part of music-making, especially of amateur music-making. It is the time when sounds are turned into music in an organized, systematic and deliberate way.

With method and structure we prepare for God the best that is possible through human endeavour. Only then can we say to the Holy Spirit, come, take it, breathe life into it.

Epilogue

Another Era

There is a gentle clunk of china as Pam comes in with the coffee tray. She can't wait to tell Dave about her fortnight in Russia. While she was away, Dave was down at 'New Life', one of the biggest Christian festivals. Fifteen of them from the church had joined ten thousand others there. 'How did it go?' asks Pam. 'It was amazing,' Dave replies, 'and the music was just so full of energy and life. We must try and get something like that going at St Peter's.' He takes a sip of coffee. 'But tell me about Russia.' 'Oh, I almost converted to Orthodoxy,' laughs Pam. 'I went into the cathedral on Easter Eve, and it was quite the most beautiful thing I have ever experienced. The singing was out of this world. All unaccompanied and yet so powerful. I brought back a recording I got out there, because I am going to see whether we can do it at St Mary's occasionally. We are all Christians', she goes on, 'and we have so much to learn from them.'

What moved Pam was the numinous quality of the orthodox music. In it, she found a spirituality which went beyond her own experience. It made its mark on her because of the sense of adoration she felt as she became drawn into an act of sacrificial worship. Dave, on the other hand, was completely caught up by the sense of unity which was forged at the festival and for which the music was in a great measure responsible.

Now that they are back at home, the efforts of their own

churches seem pale and inadequate by comparison. They have
experienced at first hand the power of music to fulfil the aims of
church worship, and naturally they want to share this with others.

Pam and Dave are both in for a disappointment. The New Life
festival happens once a year and lasts for a fortnight. They always
manage to get the top bands down there, and they have the
money to hire the best public address equipment for worship in
the big top. They can use the very latest songs and up-to-the-
minute effects which would take years to introduce to the church.
It could hardly be more different from the week by week worship
at St Peter's. In any case, the Rector does not look to the choir
principally to engender fellowship and unity. Their role is to
embellish the worship in an attitude of sacrificial offering.

Pam's hope to hear the strains of mystical orthodox music in St
Mary's is equally forlorn: they have just six singers and five instrumentalists, and no tradition of singing in this style. The Russian
choir, on the other hand, sings exclusively in that style every day,
and has a system which is dedicated to its upkeep. After years of
suppression, it is more valuable to them than ever now. The
ethereal strains are not even part of Canon Withytt's ambitions
for music at St Mary's. Unity and evangelism are his priorities.

Pam and Dave might as well be criticizing a tennis player for
failing to score goals. Yet they are not alone in muddling things
together. There are many others, in all churches, who judge music
against a standard which is different from that which was its aim.
Evangelical music is criticized for its lack of awe and divine revelation; music made in a spirit of sacrifice is chastised for its failure
to create a sense of community.

Music can never fulfil every objective of a church's life. Furthermore, everything can be achieved without it. Music is a dispensable
part of the Christian faith, the Christian religion, worship and
liturgy. So a church whose music does not foster fellowship or
evangelism, does not have to be without them. They may be ful-
filled in any number of other ways. Moreover, the capabilities of
music for worship, fellowship and evangelism often conflict. After

117

all, music cannot do everything at once. It is a precious gift, like a diamond, the hardest of stones and prized for its beauty. The gem can be used as a cutting tool, or it can be used to adorn. If it is used to incise, it is not a thing of beauty. If it is set in a ring, it is no use as a tool. Each is a legitimate use, but the same stone cannot be used for both.

What music *can* do depends upon the decisions which have been made for it and the path which has been prepared. In other words, a choice is made and a system is set up to support it. If the structure is right for the purpose, then the choice can be made to work. If a different end is decided upon, a different means must be used to reach it.

Ideally these choices should be made and understood by the whole church, or their elected representatives, even though the minister has the final say. It is important that they are choices which the whole church can own, and that they are not entirely dependent upon the enthusiasm, influence, or even skill of any one individual. Before they are turned into structures, however, they must be accepted by those who are called to live and worship within them. Here, honesty is the key.

In the early days after the review at St Mary's, a number of attempts at services and music were made under the banner of experiment. Experiment is the engine room of progress. With solid scientific foundation, it is enthusiastically to be encouraged. It consists of a hypothesis, a test and a conclusion: this might work; we will try it; has it worked – yes or no? If the answer is no, a new hypothesis is needed, and so the process continues. At St Mary's, though, things were done another way: someone hoped it might work; we let them try it; did it work? Not really, but let them do it anyway.

Margaret was the first to come forward with ideas about the music. She had had singing lessons and once hoped to be an opera singer. Her son, Tommy, was quite good on the guitar. They would lead the singing between them. It turned out that her voice was not what it once was, that she had not much grasp of the idiom of modern songs, and tended to get all the speeds wrong. But no one said anything for a year. After a few months, she had got one or two others to join her, and, by default, a system had begun to emerge. Rotas were drawn up and they had even begun to think about an outfit for them all to wear. But it was not a structure the church had chosen, and eventually something had to be said. It was only when Margaret asked for funds to buy more song-books that the truth was faced.

The new system which is about to take shape has a better chance of success. Canon Withytt has asked a group, including five Church Council members, to look into the musical needs and potential of the parish and congregation as fully as they can. They have sought opinion, found out the facts, thought and prayed about the matters in hand, and begun to formulate a philosophy which they might pursue. By the time the matter came to full council, the issues were well considered and informed. The decision to appoint a half-time director of music with certain specific duties was unanimous, and all of them have pledged their support for the new system, even though one or two had originally argued against it.

However widely accepted, though, a musical system is not itself sufficient to guarantee that the end result *will* be as intended, but only to say that it *may* be. When S. S. Wesley wrote his damning report of the state of cathedral music in the middle of the last century, many of the basic choral foundations were still intact. The provision of choristers made by the founders still held good, and the support structures of education and employment remained in place. The framework, rather, had become rusty. Beams were starting to sag, and joints beginning to come adrift.

Even the most solid structures demand upkeep and, where necessary, change. We talk sometimes of something being 'set in stone'. The implication is that it cannot be changed. In fact, structures of stone are continually changed. Buildings are extended, altered or enlarged. In churches, aisles are added, chancels and chapels tagged on. It is possible provided that the supporting walls and pillars are left untouched. Structures and systems, then, are there to be lived. They are there to organize people, and to liberate them for purposes which rest upon them.

A group of people gather to pray. But they have chosen a shaky wooden hut suspended over the edge of a cliff. As they sit down, the timbers creak and the walls begin to move. So great is the danger, that they can think of nothing but the place they are in. It completely takes over their thoughts, and their prayers are put aside. Next time, they choose an ancient stone building set into the rock. The structure which holds them is so strong that they do not think about it at all. Now they are free to pray and meditate upon the things which are away from themselves and their environment, and are of the kingdom of God.

The musical system of the church supports, holds and protects a precious gift. For some, the system has in the past obscured the gift, like an ornamental casket which is so beautiful that it surpasses the gem it is made to hold. All that has changed. In search of the nugget, the casket has been broken, and its valuable contents are left open to the wind and the rain.

Now is the time to mend the structure, and to see that that which is given of God is cared for and can flourish for the service of God. Musical systems are complex yet their results reach deep into the spiritual part of the human soul. So choices are tough. In the end, they are not to be made by people. Through prayer, these are decisions for God to make. It is for us to revere them and to keep them.

Still raise for good the supplicating voice,
But leave to heaven the measure and the choice.
(Samuel Johnson)

Appendix A

Musical Instruments and Their Ranges

1. *Stringed instruments*

The upper limits of the **violin**, **viola** and **cello** are not precisely defined, much depending upon the skill of the performer. For a player of average to good ability, the ranges given below are normal. If the player is inexperienced, the upper fifth of this range should not be used. A skilled player can reach much higher notes which can be used to good effect.

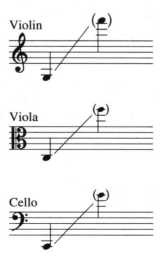

The **guitar**'s six strings are tuned: E, A, d, g, b, e. These notes sound at the pitches shown, although they are always written one octave higher for convenience.

Transpositions can be made with the use of the capo, a bar placed across all six strings in order to raise the pitch of the whole instrument.

2. Woodwind instruments

Flute

Oboe

The **B-flat clarinet** is a transposing instrument, sounding a pitch which is one tone lower than that written. This means that the whole piece is to be transposed one tone higher, so that a piece in C major is written in D major for the clarinet. The *written* pitch of the clarinet is given below.

Descant recorder

Treble recorder

3. Brass instruments

The **B-flat trumpet** is a transposing instrument, sounding a pitch which is one tone lower than that written. In preparing a trumpet part, the whole piece is to be transposed one tone higher A composition in C major, therefore, is written in D major for the trumpet. The *written* pitch of the trumpet is given below.

The **horn** (also known as French horn) is also a transposing instrument, but produces a sound which is a fifth lower than the written pitch. Because the range is large, both the treble and the bass clef are used. Sometimes when the bass clef is used, the music is written a fourth lower rather than a fifth higher than the sounding pitch. For all but the most accomplished players, the highest notes are not used. The written pitch of the horn is given below.

Appendix B

BLESSED BE THE GOD AND FATHER
ANTHEM

I Peter i. 3–5, 15–17, 22–25

COMPOSED BY

SAMUEL SEBASTIAN WESLEY.

LONDON: NOVELLO AND COMPANY, LIMITED; AND NOVELLO, EWER AND CO., NEW YORK.

125

last time. But as He which hath

call - ed you is ho - ly, so be ye ho - ly in all man-ner of con - ver -

- sa - tion; Pass the time of your so - journ-ing here in fear, in fear.

Love one a - nother with a

pure heart fer - vent-ly, See that ye love one a - no - ther,

126

128

129

G10